REFUGE

Enden për të kërkuar ushqim dhe po të jetë se nuk e gje-
jnë për të ngrënë, e kalojnë natën duke u ankuar.
Por unë do të kremtoj fuqinë tënde dhe në mëngjes do të
lëvdoj me zë të lartë mirësinë tënde, sepse ti ke qenë për
mua një kështjellë dhe një strehë ditën e fatkeqësisë.
O forca ime, ty do të këndoj lavdet, sepse ti, o Perëndi, je
kështjella ime, Perëndia që ka mëshirë për mua.
Psalmet 59:15-17 ALB

They wander about for food
And growl if they are not satisfied.

But as for me, I shall sing of Your strength;
Yes, I shall joyfully sing of Your
lovingkindness in the morning,
For You have been my stronghold
And a refuge in the day of my distress.

O my strength, I will sing praises to You;
For God is my stronghold,
the God who shows me lovingkindness.
Psalm 59: 15-17

DEDICATION AND ACKNOWLEDGMENT

Dedicated to the memory of our great friend and Christian brother

Paul Kropf

November 20, 1957 - December 25, 2010

Special thanks to everyone who helped
to bring this project to fruition:
Dr. and Mrs. Ed Holden provided wise editorial experience.
Our children, Kiffin and Kristie Ayers, Heather Dibra, Erin Oberle,
Shaun Ayers and Kristen Lane added
insightful corrections and memories.
Kiffin's expertise in formatting and layout for all
the different forms of publication was an invaluable
offering. Our entire extended family has always
provided us with love and encouragement.

Blessings to all.

Perëndia është për ne një streh dhe një forcë, një ndihmë
gjithnjë e gatshme në fatkeqësi.
Psalmet 46:1 ALB

God is our refuge and strength,
an ever-present help in trouble.
Psalm 46:1

Contents

Fore Words

The Balkan Peninsula has always experienced a turbulent history in large part due to its position on the globe and the evolution of nations over the last few millennia. It is the southern land bridge between Asia and Europe. Empires throughout history trod through these territories assuring a form of uncertainty and suspicion would permeate the people groups that lived there.

Albania, being on the Balkan Peninsula, is a place experienced with conflict, internal and external. Literally, for several millennia, the Albanians (Illyrians) have had to deal with occupation and domination by most all of the conquering empires from the Greeks and Romans through the Venetians, Bulgarians, Huns, Byzantines and Ottomans. The Balkan Peninsula provides the primary land routes from Europe to the Middle East and the Orient, the Via Egnatia and the Silk Route.

Albania was mentioned twice in the Bible. The Apostle Paul wrote in the letter to the Roman church (Romans 15:19), "So from Jerusalem all the way around to Illyricum, I have fully proclaimed the gospel of Christ." (New International Version) Illyricum was the name of the Roman province on the western side of the Balkan peninsula. Also, in his second letter to Timothy (2 Timothy 4:10), Paul wrote an update about some of the other Christian workers, "For Demas, because he loved this world, has deserted me and has gone to Thessalonica. Crescens has gone to Galatia, and Titus to Dalmatia." (NIV)

Dalmatia is a mountainous region on the eastern shore of the Adriatic Sea, in the more northern part of the Roman province of Illyricum, including parts of modern-day Albania, Montenegro and Kosova. As a point of interest and to answer a possible question, Kosova is the Albanian spelling and Kosovo is the Serbian spelling.

Since the Serbs were in power, their spelling is the more familiar to the world outside the Albanian context.

In between times of direct war and occupation, internal divisions kept the Albanians from ever developing into a strong cohesive force. After all, the Albanians descended from the Illyrians of the first and second millennia B.C.E. The Illyrians were mountain tribal people, determined survivors in a beautiful, but harsh land. Loyalties ran deep to their family or "tribe" (Fis, Albanian). The rough, mountainous terrain made wide-ranged interaction between tribes difficult and suspicions of the "unknown" impeded the development of a "corporate mentality" or even a political "kinship" except during times the various people groups had a common enemy. During the conquest of the Ottoman Empire, the otherwise disparate groups of Slavs and Illyrians fought together annually for a quarter century. That camaraderie, however, did not lead to lasting political partnerships with the other people groups. Internally, the closest thing to an enduring cohesive force between the Illyrian tribes was the Canon of Lek, an ancient code of behavior. Mountain people still refer to the kanun (pronounced kah-noon'). The tribal elders of the mountain tribes respected each other's autonomy by agreeing on social "rules".

By the mid-1990s, Albania was becoming a liberalized, fast-growing economy after years under a centrally controlled socialist economy. The fledgling financial system became dominated by Ponzi schemes, and government officials seemingly endorsed a series of pyramid investment funds because they did not interfere in their operations. Approximately two-thirds of the population invested in one or more of the nearly twenty schemes. By early 1997, the inevitable end came and the people of Albania had lost the equivalent of $1.2 billion US (out of a small population of 3 million). Fueled by their discontent at the state's failure to protect them from the fraud, the people took their protest to the streets where uncontained rioting led to looting of the weapons depots and armories nationwide and random violence. The anarchy that followed led ultimately to the toppling of the government and resulted in as many as 5,000 deaths and many thousands of injuries.

Albanian is an Indo-European language which forms its own branch in the Indo-European family and has no close relatives.

Standard Albanian has seven vowels and twenty-nine consonants. Most of the letters are pronounced as we do in English, but the chart below will help with the others. One of the characters in the story is Gjon, pronounced as we would pronounce the name John. The city Laç, for example would be pronounced as Lahch. The name Aliqe is pronounced Ah-lee′-cheh. Albania in Albanian is Shqiperia (Ship-er-ee'-a is a close English pronunciation), which means the land of the eagle, and Albanians are Shqiptar (Ship-tar').

The alphabet below is to aid you in your understanding of the occasional Albanian word you will encounter while reading.

Albanian English Pronunciation
Alphabet Symbol with Pronunciation and Example

A	a	as in far	P	p	as in pencil
B	b	as in boot	Q	tu	as in mature
C	t͡s	as in bats		(no English equivalent,	
Ç	t͡ʃ	as in chat		like German ich)	
D	d	as in drop	R	r	as in roar
Dh	ð	as in there	Rr	rr	as highly
E	ɛ	as in enter		trilled as in Spanish *burro*	
Ë	ə	as in buck	S	s	as in see
F	f	as in flee	Sh	sh	as in she
G	g	as in gulf	T	t	as in two
Gj	ɟ	as in join	Th	th	as in three
H	h	as in hot el	U	oo	as in loom
I	ee	as in see	V	v	as in value
J	y	as in yawn	X	d͡z	as in adze
K	k	as in king	Xh	j	as in Jupiter
L	l	as in alien	Y	ew	as in new
Ll	ll	as in all		(no English equivalent, like	
M	m	as in man		Turkish/Hungarian/German ü)	
N	n	as in now	Z	z	as in zone
Nj	ni	as in onion	Zh	su	as in pleasure
O	o	as in oak			

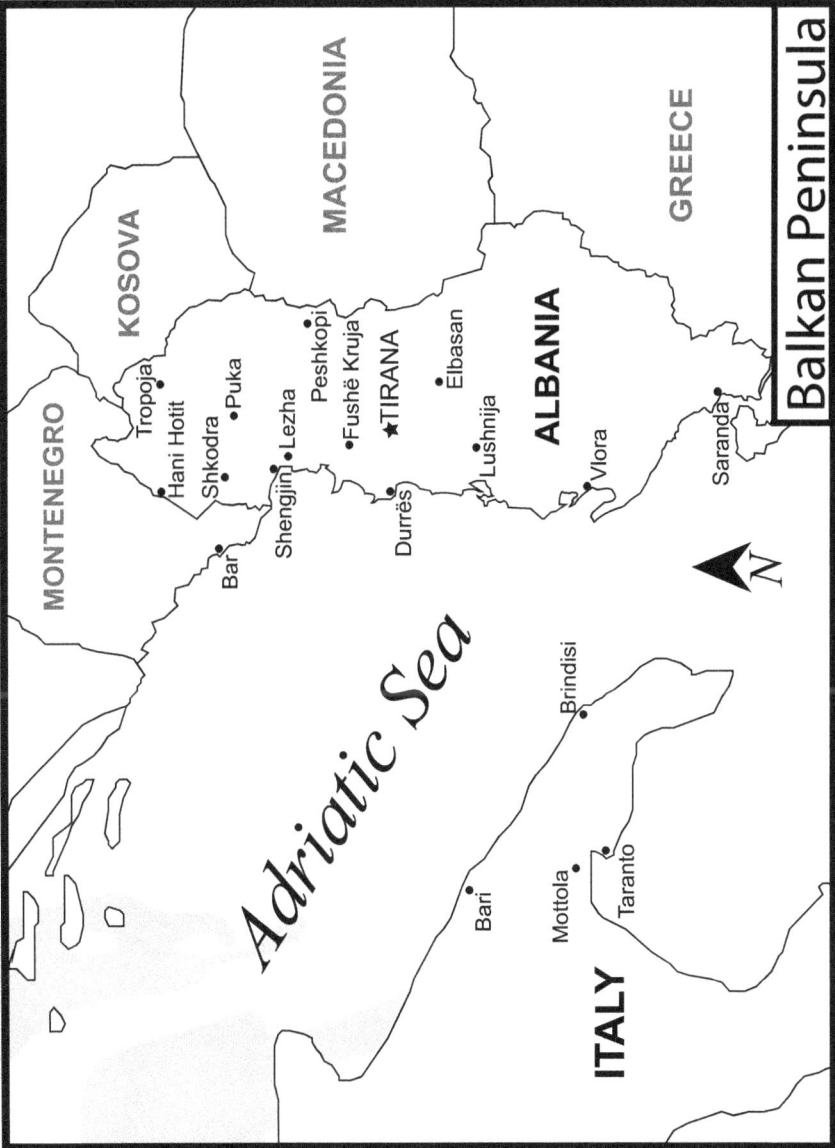

Balkan Peninsula

MONTENEGRO

KOSOVA

MACEDONIA

GREECE

Tropoja
Hani Hotit
Shkodra
Puka
Peshkopi
Shengjin Lezha
Fushë Kruja
★TIRANA
Elbasan
Lushnija
ALBANIA
Durrës
Vlora
Saranda

Bar

Adriatic Sea

N

Brindisi

Bari
Mottola
Taranto

ITALY

I. Debbie is down

Amidst random gunfire, I was approaching Debbie with the good news that we had found a place to leave the vehicles. I was looking straight at her, as she stood in the open door of our van with her back to me. It was a beautiful, sunny and cool day in March; a day that did not match the disruption of life everyone was experiencing. She was repacking a few things to hand-carry into the dock area of the port for our anticipated departure. We were told by radio that we could only take what we could carry, and be prepared to drop that and run if necessary during an evacuation.

"Oh, my God." Debbie suddenly moaned, as she collapsed backwards to the ground, unprotected in her fall.

I heard the VHF radio chatter from the front seat just a moment before. Assessing the evidence, I came to a possible conclusion that the news that came across the radio must have been really shocking to make her faint to the ground. I wondered momentarily what in the world could be that bad.

So roughly twenty meters away, Jorge, Aliqe and I rushed back to the van. We ran across the open lot hunched over, as if transversing a battle field. The shooting reverberated off the buildings making the shots seem closer and confused our orientation to the shots' origin.

I could not apply obvious direct cause to her slipping lifelessly to the dusty, rocky road. The timing with the radio was distracting, so we picked up our pace. I went directly to her easing my hand under her head.

"Are you alright?" I asked, not fully aware of the severity.

"What happened?" She murmured.

I watched it happen and still didn't know. Other questions raced in my mind, but they blurred when I saw how much blood was coming from Debbie's head. Pressure with the palm of my hand did little more than divert the blood flow over the top of my hand. Evident that this wound wasn't a scrape or bump from falling down on a rocky road, I had no immediate idea what could cause this severe a wound. I wouldn't know what caused this wound to the head by merely touching it, but I did know that the direct pressure I was applying had little effect. Forced to focus on the trauma of the moment, addressing Debbie's condition took precedent to understanding what happened.

Less than thirty minutes before, we left Debbie standing beside the van reducing and repacking what we could carry for a possible rescue, the children's things first then our things was our strategy. We brought more items than we could handle, but we thought we would be in the vehicle. Debbie had repacked the children's things and hurriedly sent them into the port area with Katie Dobbs, the children's teacher. Living in a village where there was no school for the children, we were already very thankful that our sending organization, the Cooperative Baptist Fellowship (CBF), had provided a teacher for our three school-aged children. Katie had only replaced our first teacher, Jon Harwell, six months prior. Katie was fitting nicely into the family and made a very good "older sister," especially on this day.

When the ferry left, the port workers closed the gate to the dock and went home. The guards of the Customs impoundment left. Right in front of us, the suspicions we had as we first topped the hill coming into the city this morning were coming true. Our plans to catch the last boat and wait out this turmoil in Italy were becoming bleak. We saw various military ships out in the Adriatic Sea, and even closer in, we saw the ferry out in the harbor; several hours before its scheduled departure time. It seemed to be sitting still, and its being away from the dock was not a good sign.

Katie and our children, Erin, Shaun and Kristen, had hardly gotten out of sight through a hole in the wall when Debbie went down. She expressed having had the sensation of being hit by an iron skillet and the sound in her head was like a dinner bell. Her whole body was stunned as she went to the ground. She feared she was being mugged because she had been standing there all alone with a van full of stuff and there was looting going on barely twenty meters away on the other side of the wall. Later recalling that her two main thoughts were that she needed to say something to summon help and that she wanted to hug our children. She was talking a lot to assure us and herself that she was alright. Thankfully, I was nearby and could provide the help she was summoning.

This day began with a very different plan. At this point, we were making it up as we went. We had no idea we would end up in Durrës and certainly didn't anticipate such an adventure. The inner emotional and philosophical conflict I had about leaving resolved the moment Debbie went down. I knew it was alright to leave if only for a short while.

Në rast se ngjitem në qiell, ti je atje; në rast se shtrij shtratin tim në Sheol, ti je edhe aty. Në rast se marr krahët e agimit dhe shkoj të banoj në skajin e detit, edhe aty dora jote do të më udhëheqë dhe dora jote e djathtë do të më kapë.
Psalmet 139:8-10 ALB

If I ascend to heaven, You are there;
If I make my bed in Sheol, behold, You are there.
If I take the wings of the dawn,
If I dwell in the remotest part of the sea,
Even there Your hand will lead me,
And Your right hand will lay hold of me.
Psalm 139:8-10

II. Earlier that morning

Albanian Christian Radio Network, ACRN, initiated promptly at 7:00 that morning, but we had long been up. As David Fyock, Director of the Albanian Encouragement Project (AEP), went down the roll call, many people had already left the country. Many others were making plans, as reports of increasing chaos in the north became known. We told them we would keep monitoring and let them know when we had reached Italy. Then we signed off.

Gjon Gaspri came by in a rush to tell us we needed to be going. I was really glad he came by the house. I went to see him yesterday to ask him what he thought we should do, but he was in Tirana. We spent last Saturday before with Gjon and his family at the beach, dining together and going to some of his relatives' home in Shengjin for coffee. The whole day was wonderful together. As we parted on that Saturday afternoon, we told Gjon that we trusted his judgment about when he felt it was time for us to go. Our hearts were very conflicted about going, so a trusted opinion would be welcomed.

Gjon was distraught over the situation and restated that we must leave. I could tell he was dealing with a lot of fear and disappointment. Gjon's disappointment was in part seeing us leave. He certainly understood, but we had been working together for almost three years and this year was to see some of the fruition of that work. On that level, neither of us was happy. I was able to give him a large bag of seed packets to hand out. As a matter of our friendship, he was glad we could get away from the danger. We hugged a little harder than normally as we parted and pledged to each other to get together again. Gjon was my closest Albanian friend.

Loading the van and driving away was quite an event around

our house. The neighbors were in various states of emotion. Some thought Lezha was too quiet to worry and others told us through tears to come back as soon as we could. We showed our nearby neighbors, Gjerg and Faria, how to feed the rabbits, loaded the car and said our last good-byes.

We drove away waving and smiling the best we could through our strange mix of emotions. We jostled with excitement and fear, hesitance and determination, sadness and satisfaction all jumbled up inside. Some of our neighbors shot several bursts of automatic gunfire as a goodbye salute as we crossed the railroad tracks heading toward Lezha.

We met the other two cars in town. Paul Kropf and Glenn Zimmerly were driving their vehicles with the Mennonite team. Jorge Damasceno and his wife, Hermelinda, Mel as we called her, and their baby, Venisius, were in our van.

The air was tense in Lezha. People scurried about at a faster pace than usual buying supplies. There was sporadic gunfire and many businesses were closed. And, the typical clusters of people standing around were not there. It was hard to leave as some of our believers saw us picking up these other missionaries. They ran over to say goodbye and God bless. We did write down phone numbers so we could maintain correspondence.

Before we left town, we got two independent reports that the trouble had broken out in Shkodra. There were already four dead and twenty-eight injured in Shkodra and the town was out of control. Thugs were blocking the bridge across the Buna River and also taking control of the border crossing at Hani Hotit. For weeks, we had heard scary news from the southern border crossing at Kakavij near Gjirokaster about armed gangs taking control of the border and several people having been killed. The gangs were asking for payment to pass and if Hani Hotit was anything like that, it would be way too risky. We reluctantly decided to go toward Durrës even though we didn't know what we'd find.

Just before we drove south, we got another report of a road block just five miles to the north, large numbers of people being killed and injured, stores being looted in Shkodra, prisoners being released and the newly restored Catholic church being burned.

Among the prisoners released was Fatos Nano, one of the

last communist leaders. Needless to say, we were getting a little nervous at this point. We checked back in with Dave Fyock, ACRN, to let him know we were changing our plans. We would continue to keep him posted of road conditions and any situations along the way to Durrës. That was our only way out at this point. The airport had officially been closed now and we didn't know what to expect in any direction.

On the radio, we were hearing rumors of roadblocks near the airport and traffic jams. Every town and village on our route, including the airport area, was uneventful. There were very few cars, most businesses were closed and there were very few people wanting rides to Tirana. We saw no police or military and there were no roadblocks, legal or otherwise. We saw armloads of guns and ammunition being taken towards the villages, with some even being carried by children. There were loads of flour and grain being carted by horse and buggies. There were hordes of men and boys along the roadside pregnant with anticipation, waiting for something to happen.

Ti më ke hetuar, o Zot, dhe më njeh.
Ti e di kur ulem dhe kur ngrihem,
ti e kupton nga larg mendimin tim.
Ti e shqyrton me kujdes ecjen time dhe pushimin tim dhe i
njeh thellë të gjitha rrugët e mia.
Sepse, edhe para se të jetë fjala mbi gojën time ti,
o Zot, e di atë plotësisht.
Ti më rrethon nga pas dhe përpara
dhe vë dorën tënde mbi mua.
Psalmet 139:1-5

O LORD, you have searched me and you know me. You
know when I sit and when I rise; you perceive my thoughts
from afar. You discern my going out and my lying down; you
are familiar with all my ways. Before a word is on my tongue
you know it completely, O LORD. You hem me in--behind
and before; you have laid your hand upon me.
Psalm 139:1-5

III. The ride to the hospital

Debbie's coherency was a relief in the midst of my frustrating efforts to stop the bleeding. Pressure wasn't helping, so I repositioned my hands and pulled Debbie's head more tightly against my chest. Nothing seemed to change.

Back in the States prior to Albania, Debbie facilitated individuals with traumatic brain injuries (TBI) in a work rehabilitation setting. From this experience, her worst nightmares were to have a head injury and need to go to the hospital in Albania.

Silently to herself, she was going through the basic orientation questions she had used many times with her clients. "What is my name? What day is this? Where am I?" Inside, she found encouragement from knowing all of the answers. Outside, she kept talking so we'd know she was still with us.

Our good friend and Mennonite missionary colleague, Paul Kropf, had jumped in his vehicle and pulled up beside us. It was evident that the wound needed medical attention. Now, both parts of Debbie's nightmare were coming true, a head injury and a hospital visit. Debbie and I shuffled like in an awkward dance, the evacuation waltz, toward the open passenger-side back door of Paul's car. Allen Umble, one of Paul's teammates, opened the door as Paul looked back over the front seat. He exclaimed, "Get in!"

"Do you know where the hospital is?" He continued.

I had been to Durrës many times, but had never noticed the hospital. "No," was all that came out of my mouth even though I normally would have given a longer answer. The former communists blended medical and military buildings among the residential areas, which were primarily four or five story apartment buildings that all looked alike. Regardless of where it is, we knew to start going toward the turnoff from the main road into the port area in order to get back into town. That was the direction Paul had pointed his vehicle.

As I was answering Paul's question and we were trying to orient ourselves to get in the car, we suddenly noticed an Albanian man standing next to the front passenger-side window less than two feet away. No one had noticed him walking up, but we were focused on Debbie's bleeding head. His being there seemed odd, mainly because he was the only Albanian within view. As a people, they are very helpful in times of crises and are not shy to jump in and help. Generally, a crowd would gather and a more likely scenario would be too many too close. Not today. The looting of the armory and random gunfire had sent most everyone inside.

Paul didn't skip a beat and immediately asked in Albanian, "Do you know where the hospital is?"

Immediately he answered, "Yes"!

"Can you go with us and show the way?" Paul retorted.

He answered, "Pa tjetër" (Of course), as he slid into the front seat and immediately looked over his left shoulder to watch us settle in the back.

Debbie had been hesitant to get in Paul and June's back seat because she was dripping blood. She knew it would have to be cleaned. With the loving, but firm word from a close friend, Paul said, "Don't worry about that, Debbie! We'll clean it later." We had completed our awkward entrance trying to ignore the fact we were dripping blood on the seat.

After our door closed, Paul verified with our newly acquired Albanian guide that we were to head toward the entrance of the port.

"Yes, go that way," the guide confirmed.

Even though there were things happening that took precedent over the normal formalities, later, I felt bad that I didn't even ask for this particular Albanian's name. I don't even remember looking him square in the eyes as I normally do. I remember thinking it odd that he was even there. His being out in the open seemed brave to me considering most everyone else had gone inside unless they were wielding a Kalashnikov.

Our Albanian guide was about my height, five feet nine inches, had a two or three-day growth of beard and a typical full head of hair. Albanians usually had really nice hair, so I noticed nothing unusual about this man's appearance, although observing him with my peripheral vision. I tried to keep pressure on Debbie's wound without smothering her as we started on our way.

Allen was praying out loud as got in and drove away. "Father God, we love and praise you and call to you now for your…," trailed his voice at our departure.

Barely fifty meters outside the port's entry and before we gained any appreciable speed, a three-meter high concrete block wall began on our left side. The wall separated the rail yard from the vehicle traffic of the port. There was a gaping hole in the wall near its beginning. It appeared that some large vehicle, perhaps a truck of some kind, had barged through. Barely five years since the fall of communism, broken down structures were still common. We didn't notice it as we drove in earlier that morning, but it clearly had been that way for a while.

Pointing toward the opening in the wall, our guide leaned across Paul and said in Albanian with a hurried tone, "Turn here!".

On the other side, there were piles of rubble that looked like masonry debris and miscellaneous scrap iron that had been piled up beside the railroad tracks. There's no way to know how long they'd been there, but this obviously wasn't a place to drive.

Paul said, "Are you sure?!"

"Yes, go! Go!" The guide pointedly encouraged.

Carefully, Paul turned into the field and maneuvered around the piles of rubble as our guide signaled course corrections to get us to our goal, an actual street. I halfway expected someone from the train station to take notice of our encroachment, emerge from the station and offer some verbal objection, but none came. In just a few minutes, we were out on the main road.

We entered the city street on the side of the traffic circle in front of the train station. We knew that traffic circle well. I was stopped there once by a policeman that didn't like the way I went around the circle. We often joked that the officer just needed some money for a coffee. Also, one of our favorite pizza places in Durrës was just off the circle. We loved their artichoke heart pizza because it was the only unusual topping they offered, and it came without the egg on top. Pizza was still a developing art in 1997. It seemed most pizza places didn't know which model to follow, Italian, American, European, or Albanian, whatever that turned out to be. I mentally flashed through these thoughts of the pizza stand and the policeman as we bumped off the curb and sped west down the coast road. It placed me on the map in my mind offering some comfort knowing where we were.

Getting up our speed on that road, I remember our guide looking over his left shoulder toward us in the back seat and then turning forward as he said, "Spejt! Spejt! Më spejt!" (Faster! Faster! Even faster!)

"I'm going as fast as I can." Paul said, going as fast as he could under the circumstances, while steadily blowing his horn.

As we sped by, I noticed a lady on the sidewalk with her young son. She was keeping her son, who looked to be five or six years old, tucked as closely as possible between her legs as they hurried down the street to safety. She was using herself to shield the boy, which made them shuffle as awkwardly as Debbie and I had just a few minutes before. Pondering momentarily the dire situation in the country, I thought how Albania had seemingly been doing so well in their redevelopment. Now, most Albanians were just as confused by the events of these last several months as we expatriates were. The ones that weren't confused or angry were having fun shooting their automatic weapons into the air.

Our guide gave instruction to Paul as we neared intersections. For four, maybe five, blocks he had given the keep going straight signal, with his fingers together all facing forward and shaking his hand up and down. I kept my focus on Debbie and kept my mental prayer posture oriented toward God. Finally, at one intersection, he said, "Turn right at the next road." We did, only slowing slightly, upsetting our balance in the back seat. After two more blocks, he said, "Turn left for a block and then the hospital is on the right." Sure enough, there it was.

Debbie was still conscious and the bleeding seemed to have slowed a bit. "Praise the Lord!" I jubilated!

As we drove up onto the gravel driveway of the hospital, our guide called out the window in Albanian to the guard, "An American woman has been shot." Paul asked, "What do you want me to do?" As we were getting out of the back seat, the policeman that was guarding the hospital motioned to us from the protection of the overhang of the entry way. He was afraid to venture out in the open.

I took a mental note of the real peace I felt inside. It was a little counter intuitive, maybe, but I felt that inner peace that's hard to explain in such situations. In case we had to be left behind, I knew the children would be taken care of by all the other missionaries. All of the CBF team currently in the country was there on the dock and we knew dozens of others there that were happy to help if it came to that. We had already been in radio contact with the dock for several hours so we were confident about the children.

"Just send our passports back up here to us. We've probably missed the rescue. I'm sure the Lord will help us sort it out. Soften the story to the children and we'll be in touch with you as soon as we can." We resolved to Paul. In that, we did not want to be left in the country without our passports.

Paul nodded as our guide sat quietly in the front seat listening. Then, they drove away as Debbie and I resumed our awkward dance toward medical help. In all of this, I forgot to thank our helper.

After having stepped out of the car, I noticed how much louder the munitions sounded as the bangs echoed around the hospital and the apartment buildings next door. No wonder the guard was playing it safe as he waved us into the shelter and then rushed to open the door into the emergency room. Those inside directed us straight in to a triage room. No paperwork. No questions.

We were led into a room with a hard metal bed in the middle that was surrounded by bloody bandages from earlier patients. Debbie was helped up on the table face down and the doctors cut some hair from around the wound, put a patch on it and sent us to get an x-ray. Holding on to a still-bleeding Debbie, we walked toward a dank, dark, dirty room that resembled a storeroom more than an X-ray room. The technician told Debbie to lay with her head back on a specific spot, which was not even close to possible. This would put her directly on her wound. Debbie agreed to try if the technician would hurry really fast. The tech agreed and headed to the machine as Debbie lay back with help. Probably to our advantage, there was no electricity. He gave the standard answer, "After five minutes, it will come." We had already heard the power had been off since nine that morning. Debbie was on the verge of passing out. It was evident she was working hard to remain conscious.

About that time, Debbie said, "Come hold me. I'm about to lose it."

As I was strengthening my grip on Debbie, Jorge came rushing in and hastily said in English, "Quick, Brian is calling you on the radio!" He took over holding Debbie and I hurried outside.

Jorge took hold of Debbie and I ran back out to the van to answer the radio. Thankfully an Albanian from the hospital was guarding the van, although sitting in the driver's seat smoking. We don't allow smoking in the van and the Albanians always respected our wishes, but I wasn't about to reprimand him under the circumstances. I jumped into the front passenger seat and grabbed the radio.

"8-Golf, 8-Golf, this is 3-4-Bravo"

"Hey! This is 8-Golf. Go ahead," Brian replied.

"Jorge said someone called. I just wanted to check in and let you all know Debbie is being cared for, but there is no electricity. Over."

"I copy. We'll keep praying. Just keep us informed about every five or ten minutes. Over. "

"Roger. 3-4-Bravo clear." I put down the radio and headed back into the hospital. It was about 3:20 PM by my watch.

Debbie told Jorge she wasn't sure she could hold on much longer. She'd lost lots of blood, she was dizzy and her head was really hurting. No sooner had she said that to Jorge, Debbie felt surrounded by brightness. Everything seemed so peaceful and serene and clean. She was in total comfort.

But, only for a moment until she heard Jorge calling her back, "Debbie, Debbie, Debbie!" It all seemed very surreal, so the medical staff decided to abandon this phase and move on. The doctors waved off the x-ray and called us back up front.

They brought in what they called a stretcher, but it looked more like a lawn chair without straps. It was just a frame with wide gaps over which they draped a blanket. I came back in the room as Debbie said, "I have to sit up. I can't lie on this." It was evident the stretcher was not going to happen. So, Jorge and I got on either side of Debbie to help her walk back to the first triage room. As we slowly returned to the room, Jorge and Debbie told me about what happened while I was outside.

*Mos harroni mikpritjen, sepse disa duke
e praktikuar e priten pa ditur engjëj!
Hebrenjve 13:2 ALB*

*Do not forget to entertain strangers,
for by so doing some people have entertained angels
without knowing it.
Hebrews 13:2*

IV. Back on the dock

Paul and our guide bumped out of the hospital's gravel driveway heading back to the port. Paul was pondering and praying to himself as both of them rode along without conversation. Paul had many things coursing through his mind; Debbie's situation and the order of duties to perform upon returning to the dock were most acute. He and June were also responsible for the safety of the YES Team, as they were their supervising missionaries.

As Paul approached the dock, he saw Jorge standing next to our van. He had assumed guard duty after we rushed off to the hospital. The gates were still closed and the only signs of life were the few people standing outside the entrance beside the vehicles they guarded.

Slowing the car as he got up to Jorge, Paul called out the window. Before the car had stopped completely, he said to Jorge "Take their passports back up to the hospital." Paul turned to thank our guide for his help, but he was gone. Surprised, or maybe better, shocked, because he neither heard the door open nor sensed the movement of someone getting out of the vehicle. Paul quickly scanned the driveway for a glimpse of our helper. He was nowhere to be seen. It was a wide-open driving area at the entrance of the ferry docks and there were no crowds or physical barriers close enough for him to hide behind. Especially, in the very short moment Paul had looked away.

Paul was stunned because he immediately felt certain that he had been sitting in the front seat with an angelic provision. God had provided exactly what we needed in the exact moment we needed it. He nervously parked the car and didn't mention it to anyone until he was back inside the dock with June. Paul and June guarded their secret while they processed it in their minds and hearts; all the while praising God.

Inside the locked gates of the dock, there was a numbing anxiety surrounding their inner sense that God was somehow in control. This had an interestingly calming effect. This anxiety related to several factors. Firstly, Debbie's wound. This reality demonstrated another factor of concern, the vulnerability everyone faced with all of the erratic shooting. The expats were all out in the open, and merely grouped beside a three-meter wall that defined only a single side of the staging area of the dock. Thirdly, the fearful waiting of the ones trying to escape as they watched the looting and removal of vehicles from the Custom's impound straight across from the staging area. They wondered if they would be the next targets and prayed for rescuing.

Katie, Erin, Shaun and Kristen had made it out to the collection of expats. Carrying their little bags and oblivious to what had happened, the kids walked toward the dock. The missionaries that had been tipped off about Debbie's wound saw them coming and made a point to draw them into the fold and care for them. They engaged the children while someone took Katie aside and explained what had happened. She was asked to keep it from the kids until word came back from the hospital.

The women and children were strategically positioned beside a vehicle and along a wall that adjoined the rear bumper. This L-shaped barrier provided partial protection and some peace of mind. As a precaution, the men stood around the vehicle and arced to the wall around the women and children forming a perimeter. Today's events were so unpredictable that no one knew what to expect next. Especially, in light of what they were observing, across the way in the Custom's lot where trucks were unloaded and goods carted away, and vehicles being hot-wired and lost in the tumult.

No vehicles could leave the compound, because the gate was locked earlier when the port workers left. Items were extracted from the area if they could be handed through the hole in the wall or passed through the gate; that was until someone broke in and hot-wired a concrete truck that was being brought into the country. It was the first one I'd ever heard of in Albania. Most all concrete is mixed on the ground and manually moved in buckets to where it is needed; a concrete mixer truck was a huge step forward.

The truck was started and the driver practiced operating the large truck within the limits of the dock staging area. The foreigners waiting on the dock were all terrified that the novice driver would lose control and barrel into the crowd. It was a very stressful few minutes while the driver drove circles around the dock area with several of his friends clinging to various parts of the mixer. When he gained confidence, he headed for the closed gate. Wham! He hit the gate breaking the lock and provided escape to the dozens of other vehicles unfortunate enough to be retained in the Customs lot. Like a convoy, the parking lot emptied, driven by whoever was "clever" or assertive enough to end up with a vehicle.

Missionaries and other foreign workers alike were both relieved of some of the immediate dangers and apprehensive to what an open gate might invite. Everyone was in the country because we loved the Albanian people and had a vested interest in helping them physically and spiritually. We understood the political and social upheaval we were experiencing in the country, and didn't let that affect our relationships with the people with whom we worked. Today, something was different. At least for me, I was partially afraid of the people. This surprised me.

Perhaps, it was a fear of the unknown and accompanying unpredictability. No, this was different. Unpredictability was "normal" for life in Albania. In our nearly four years in Albania, we became very comfortable with the erratic and verging on chaotic world in which we lived. We transcended scary situations before, and never did we transfer whatever happened categorically to "all" the people of Albania.

Standing exposed on the dock with no apparent way out, except for the now open gate that hung there like a lure, this event became unique. We knew we would have to be rescued if we were to leave. As the day wore on, the stories of how everyone found their way to the dock made it seem even more special. One story after another described how the Lord had opened and closed exit routes directing us all to a relatively safe place, together. We mostly all had started out in another direction, but found ourselves making our way to Durrës.

*Sepse është shkruar: "Ai do t'u urdhërojë engjëjve
të vet rreth teje të të ruajnë.
Luka 4:10 ALB*

For it is written: 'He will command his angels concerning
you to guard you carefully';
Luke 4:10 (*Psalm 91:11)*

V. Why didn't we see this coming?

"How could we have been so oblivious?" I wondered to myself this afternoon as we waited at the hospital and later this evening at the dock. Tuesday, two days ago, we were sure that it would be no problem for us to stay in the country and the trouble would surely die down. The few times we spoke with family back in the States, we attempted to calm their fears. All they saw on television was footage from the anarchy in the southern cities, which was bad. On the contrary, we had seen nothing but calm.

The CBF team had met in Tirana to discuss the growing situation. We consulted to see if there was anything we needed to do to help one another on the team and to inform Atlanta of our statuses. We determined that everyone had an exit plan with multiple alternatives. No one thought they would have to activate the extra plans, but it was absolutely prudent to have them. Some were going north, some east and some west. I had my doubts about the east plan, because it required traveling south for a ways and then east. That was very close to some of the areas that were unstable, but that couple felt it would be safe.

One of the plans was for the rest of the team in Tirana to come up to Lezha and wait with us for the unrest to wane. Anarchy had been raging in the south for at least two months, but we all doubted the trouble would come past Tirana. If it did, then we could all go across the northern border into Montenegro. We performed under the assumption that the instability would follow the typical south to north pattern we had seen.

Two members of our church in Lezha and our pastor, Jorge Damasceno, were accompanying me to Tirana that day. Each of us had gone for different reasons and to different meetings so we compared notes later as we returned north. I remember the confident resolve I felt as we began the drive home.

Our CBF team met in the basement of the Stephen Center, located across from the Baptist Center. It was a favorite place to eat and the food was reminiscent of America, and especially because the coffee was great. In most places, we had the choice of espresso, Turkish, or cappuccino. The espressos were nice, but very "short." Turkish coffee was nice for us hard-core coffee drinkers, but it also is fairly short and you have to drink the coffee through the grounds. Cappuccinos, on the other hand, were the closest thing to a "long" cup of coffee and they were cheap, usually the equivalent to fifty cents. We never drank them in the States because they were so expensive. Also, the Stephen Center was the only place in Tirana to get a large mug of American coffee.

When our meetings involved everyone on the team, we tried to time them to involve lunch at the Stephen Center. Meetings were usually late in the morning or early afternoon. This gave the Earls and us time to get there, since we lived the farthest away. The Earls lived in Kruja and we were in Lezha, both about an hour and a half to two hours away. We meet, eat, and get home before dark. Often, even short distances took a long time to transverse, so we tried to be cautious. Besides, there was a nationwide curfew at dark.

Shelia and Arville were out of the country so they weren't at the meeting on Tuesday. Those of us that met were Darrell and Kathy Smith, Rick and Martha Shaw, Tony and Ricki Buesing, Mary Ida, and I. The Smith and Shaw children were there with us. Debbie and the family had stayed at home to do school work and general preparation should something happen.

Our general feeling was one of trying to sort out the conflicting signals we were getting from our hearts, the embassies and what we saw on the street. The embassies were issuing the generic "all non-essential personnel should leave the country" warnings. Of course, no missionary would consider themselves "non-essential," so that message didn't get much traction with us. We assumed the embassies were most likely responding to the anarchy in the southern districts and didn't apply as much to us. What we were experiencing in our arena was nothing like that.

We all had our plans, but no one was interested in using them.

Each family had communicated their exit plans with the team and the office in Atlanta. The home office was leaving it up to us since we were closest to the situation. We were all glad we were with CBF. The missionaries with the International Mission Board of the Southern Baptist Convention had been forced by their organization to leave the next day, Wednesday. Gale Hartley and I had coffee before my CBF team meeting and we agreed it seemed excessively early. He even expressed a slight feeling of embarrassment to be "bailing out," as he put it. As it turned out, however, they were among the last to get out of the country on commercial transport.

In spite of the dire events in southern Albania, we left the meeting that day resolved to sit tight and to stay in the country. Mary Ida had tickets to London for a later date, but decided at the meeting to change the date and go ahead. She left the next day. Everyone with me in the van that day was feeling the trouble would get to Tirana and fizzle out. We started home confident in that belief.

Just in case the north destabilized, I withdrew some cash from the bank. Those of us in Lezha to the north had a plan to go out a northern border crossing point. Hani Hotit being the closest border crossing to us, yet still three hours away. We'd drive up through Shkodra to Hani Hotit, cross into Montenegro and drive to the port city of Bar. From Bar, we would catch a regularly scheduled ferry to Bari, Italy and wait out the unrest.

In our minds, if we had to leave, we pictured a leisurely "field trip" to Italy, for a couple of weeks. The kids could do school work while we practiced our Italian and took a "break" until things settled down. Reflecting back, I wondered, "what kind of illusion was that?"

As we drove through Fushë Kruja, about half way home, a military officer in plain clothes flagged us down. We noticed the Army troop truck some distance in front of us. I was driving, so I watched the truck kick up dust as we all dodged the normal mix of animals, people and vehicles sharing the highway. Other than that, I'd paid it little to no attention. The officer saw our Lezha tags and flagged us down as he spoke on his radio.

The officer was standing beside two army trucks loaded with half-uniformed soldiers. These trucks were carrying some of the draftees from the north that had been sent to Vlora, where the trouble all started. He said the soldiers were getting a five-day break and asked if a soldier could catch a ride with us to his village just outside Lezha. We gladly added him to our group.

All of us being fluent in Albanian, we were interested in getting his perspective on what was going on in the country. It is very seldom that we got a chance to carry on a private conversation with someone in the military, especially during this trying time in Albania. It was a blessing to have this opportunity alone with a soldier.

We opened the van door, which accentuated the dust and noise of that busy junction in the road. Climbing in with all his gear and automatic weapon, as we introduced ourselves informally, this young twenty-five year old soldier named Mirim sat in the middle seats. The other riders made room for him. Jorge and I were in the front. Our attention immediately focused on Mirim.

"Eight died from Puka, seventeen from Tropoja," he said. "We couldn't shoot back," he followed with noticeable emotion in his voice. We were curious about the fate of volunteers from other areas of the north, but decided not to ask.

"Why did you volunteer to fight'?" we asked.

"For my president," he continued, "but I agree with the opposition forces."

"If you agree with the opposition, why are you fighting for the President?"

"They are paying us 40,000 Lekë a month. Now, we have a few days to rest."

We hated to think this young man's life was being put at risk for 400 US dollars per month, especially since he didn't have passion for the cause only a salary, a small one at that. Dying in battle is always terrible, but this seemed especially wasteful. We couldn't become involved other than to pray, so we all refrained from offering our personal editorials.

As this brave young man shared more of his experiences leading up to this short visit home, we began to sense the condition of the country was much graver than we had let ourselves believe. These military units were given weapons without ammunition to show force, but without the possibility to respond to potential backlash from this type of instigation. Mirim, and the other survivors were getting a brief liberty at home before they had to report for duty again. Some of the dead had been in the military less than a month.

Mirim and others like him were in the first wave of draftees. They were a calculated risk. Mirim was one of the lucky ones thus far. At least twenty-five others were not so lucky. In less than a month, they had been drafted, outfitted and killed. Up until that point, I felt like the conflict was far away. Suddenly, it seemed next door.

Many of the people in the north had refused to go voluntarily. So many refused to go, that even with the draft, the government had to back down from its initially aggressive posture and offer a monetary incentive to join. The north was known for its blood feuds, and now blood had been let. And, according to the Canon of Lek Dukegjini, it allowed for revenge.

I paused the van a moment as we bid goodbye to Mirim and promised him our prayers. We watched him walk toward his home in his small village of Tresh. As some of the villagers recognized him and began to respond, we continued on our way northbound on the national highway thankful that Mirim was safe at home, for now. The five miles that remained in our trip home were quite different from the first five. Conversation was more solemn and addressed the "what next" of our plans that had just moved from static to evolving. We all questioned what would be the north's posture now that some of its young men had died for apparently no productive or honorable reasons.

Unfortunately, our resolve to stay was crumbling. We knew these latest developments didn't bode well for our area, but we were still extremely conflicted about the decision to go. Leaving our Albanian friends, especially in the church, was very difficult. It felt as we were disserting them, negating all we had taught them about the power and presence of an omnipotent, miracle-working God. We felt that leaving was showing a lack of faith, a faith we'd preached about for several years.

I dropped Jorge at his pallati, an apartment building, and we made a plan to discuss our exit strategy after we talked with our wives. I headed out toward our house in Ishull Lezha trying to organize all the thoughts spinning in my head so I could unpack them in some coherent way. I was to bring Debbie up to speed with all that had just happened.

When I got home, Debbie and I talked about the situation and for the first time began to work through readying to leave. Generally, we were still reasonably comfortable with our own situation in Lezha, but decided to be prepared just in case we decided to leave after speaking with Jorge and Paul. We tuned in to the BBC World Service on the HF radio for an update. That's when we got the first word that trouble had broken out in Tropoja. Tropoja was the birthplace of the president and they were staunch supporters. The news was unclear as to the nature of the trouble in that area. We pondered the question "Was the unrest for or against the President?" It was a pertinent question noticing how fast the north had responded to its dead sons. The next news byte said two other northern cities Peshkopi and Bulqiz had trouble as well.

"Trouble" over the last few weeks had begun with the breaking in and looting of the armory at a military installation. Arms and ammunition would be handed out freely as far as it would go. People would excitedly haul their prizes off toward home and hurriedly learn to load and fire their new weapons. The pattern then was to go out into the streets and fire wildly into the air for hours and hours. Millions of rounds of ammunition were expended like this. Dozens of people were either wounded or killed as a result of this style of fracas. That same thing was happening in these northern cities, but it was still unclear which side they were on. We all still wanted to stay in the country if at all possible.

If these incidences were of the Northerners flexing their muscles in support of the government and against the Socialist opposition in the south, we would still be safe temporarily where we were. The modus operandi looked so much like what we had been observing in the south, that we were beginning to lose our confidence in a speedy solution.

Tuesday night, we went to bed praying fervently for the situation and feeling more resolved that we should plan to leave the country for a week or two until order was restored.

Por ai iu përgjigj atyre dhe tha: "Në mbrëmje ju thoni: "Do të jetë mot i mirë, sepse qielli është i kuq".
Dhe në mëngjes thoni: "Sot do të jetë stuhi, sepse qielli është i kuq dhe i vranët". Hipokritë, pra, ju dini të dalloni dukuritë e qiellit, por nuk arrini të kuptoni shenjat e kohës?
Mateu 16:2-3 ALB

But [Jesus] replied to them, "When it is evening, you say, 'It will be fair weather, for the sky is red.'"And in the morning, 'There will be a storm today,
for the sky is red and threatening.'
Do you know how to discern the appearance of the sky but cannot discern the signs of the times?
Matthew 16:2-3

VI. Treatment at last

I was intrigued by Debbie's story of seeing the brightness and her feeling of peacefulness, comfort and cleanliness as we walked back to the treatment room. Since, that was so not what surrounded her, I was sorry I wasn't there for her when that happened.

We mazed our way back toward where we entered the hospital. During this whole ordeal, everything was seemingly open to the public. If someone wanted to peek in or stand around and watch, it seemed to be okay. The main doctor arrived, and we met with him in the first room we had upon our arrival. So, Debbie got back onto the hard table lying face down with her hands under her face. I was increasingly thankful that I was there with her.

More hair was cut, which gave a clearer view of the trauma, so the doctor could take a closer examination of the wound. It clearly was two holes, an entry and an exit. It wasn't yet evident if there was any internal damage to the skull, but first indicators were that the bullet had passed on through near the surface. This was quite a feat considering the bullet went between the scalp and the skull, in and out in the span of an inch, without fragmenting the bone. After the doctor pushed and prodded to make sure there were no bullet or bone fragments, and he injected something to numb the area. He then proceeded to cut between the two holes and with his finger he felt again inside the wound.

Warm blood poured down Debbie's face and hands as it dripped onto the table in front of her face. Debbie asked me several times to wipe it from her eyes. The only thing I had was a handkerchief in my pocket, so I pulled it out and attempted to wipe her eyes clean. At one point, the doctor reached over and took our handkerchief out of my hand and used it to wipe a spot. When he finished, he gave the handkerchief to the other doctor and he rinsed it off in the sink and brought it back to me. I felt a slight sense of purpose that I was able to contribute something to the treatment, and tremendously appreciative that the doctors allowed me to remain with Debbie.

Some of the time during the procedure, I stood beside Debbie with my hand on her back and my eyes closed, praying. After a minute or so, I felt a hand on my arm and I looked up to see all the doctors looking at me and said, "You can sit over there." They thought I was getting sick. I declined, saying "I'm fine. I was praying for Debbie, but also for you and Albania." They smiled and went back to work. I kept praying with my eyes open so they wouldn't worry. I wanted them to concentrate on Debbie.

The main doctor began to sew up the wound. "Ouch!" Debbie winced as they put in the last stitches. They seemed to hurt worse than the others.

The doctor told Debbie, "You have a hard head."

She remarked to him, "Yes, I do, just like the Albanians." He laughed and Debbie continued, "I guess I'm a sister now."

"Yes, that's right," he said smiling and appreciating a little levity in his day.

The doctor and his assistant poured a little warm water on Debbie's head and began to rub her hair and clean off her face with a little piece of gauze. Her hands and the table were covered with globs of blood, and between her fingers were big clots. It was surreal, but it felt good to have her wound closed.

Now, with this part over, it was time to wrap the bandage around Debbie's head. Someone had come up and laid a roll of gauze on the table as the doctors were cleaning her head. They didn't notice that they had put the gauze partially in the puddle of blood. The doctor picked up the role and began to wrap Debbie's head without any notice taken that he was leaving random red blotches around her head. When he finished, he said, "There," like he'd finished a masterpiece. She definitely now looked the part of a war victim. To look at her, one couldn't tell that there was just one wound or where it was. We weren't about to complain; concerned that it would slow our exit.

They lead us to a recovery room, and motioned toward one of the three beds. Debbie was quickly trying to decide which one of the beds was the least dirty, and Jorge had since returned. I filled out some forms, and then joined the discussion about painkillers and I.V.s that Jorge and the medical folks were already having. Debbie was having trouble hearing our conversation because of the loud ringing in her ears, but, although muffled, she heard enough to say no way to an I.V. We had no plans staying any longer than necessary, which definitely included not being tied to something.

They gave Debbie something in the hip for pain, and we were on our way to rejoin the group at the port to await any possible rescue. There was no mention of payment as we left. When we got to the hospital exit door, there was a loud shot nearby. Debbie hesitated a little and then we headed for the van arm-in-arm, confident God would get us through this ordeal somehow.

Another victim of a shooting was being rushed into the hospital, as we stepped out of the building. Debbie commented about this being the first of many. We all wished it wasn't so, and we agreed that this unfortunate situation would produce many victims, of which we felt blessed that Debbie's wound wasn't any worse.

Unë e kërkova Zotin, dhe ai m'u përgjigj
dhe më çliroi nga të gjitha tmerret e mia.
Psalmet 34:4 ALB

"I sought the Lord, and He heard me,
and delivered me from all my fears."
Psalm 34:4

VII. Back to the Dock

Jorge drove, while I sat in the back with Debbie to help steady her. Having someone hitch a ride was normal in Albania, so one of the guards from the hospital rode with us. The guard may have lived on that side of town, or it was just in his direction. We didn't discuss his plan, but having him along was no trouble and even seemed natural. Jorge picked a smooth route back to the port for Debbie's sake. It was a good feeling to be able to radio back to the port that Debbie was okay, and we were on our way.

"8-Golf, 8-Golf, this is 3-4-Bravo." I called out.

"This is 8-Golf. Go ahead," Brian came back.

"Just to let you know Debbie is doing well and we're on our way back to the port. Over."

"Great to hear! The gate is open now so you can drive out to where we are. We are two Land Rovers to your right against the wall. Over."

"Roger, we'll be there in a few minutes. Over and Clear."

"8-Golf clear." Brian followed.

Upon arrival back at the port, just as they said, the gate was standing wide open. There were no police or military present. We drove directly into the dock area, past Glenn Zimmerly's car and the Bethany Services van where we were parked. Slowly picking our way through the crowds of people curiously lingering, awaiting some random opportunity that might present itself. These opportunities could be something to abscond or a ride with whomever comes to pick up the foreigners. There were more people on the dock than I had imagined. This added to my amazement of how fast news travels in this country.

As soon as we stopped the van, some of the expats anxiously motioned for us to move the vehicles from around the group as quickly as possible. That momentarily tainted the joy of our arrival, but I understood they were still on edge because of what had been happening. It hadn't been too long since the episode with the concrete truck churning up the fear of the crowd, and then busting through the gate. Later, some of the men told us how they had gotten a kick out of the comedic antics of the guys that were trying to hang on to the truck's chute and running boards as the driver wildly wheeled around the dock paying no attention to anyone. That was what added to the horror. This happened in the midst of all the people scattered around the dock. Now that the Customs lot was completely empty, the group didn't want to draw attention to our crowd. So, we moved quickly.

Tony took Debbie to a place he and others prepared for her when she returned. Everyone was standing or sitting outside the two vehicles originally bound for the ferry, which were backed in against the concrete block wall. As you sit in the car, the water was off to the right about thirty meters. Most of the foreigners were on the waterside of the cars. Many had found cardboard to sit on as they leaned against the wall. Debbie was in the back seat of the Land Rover that was being used like a command center.

With Brian's radio in the car, sounds became much more of a focus to Debbie. Through the ringing in her ears, Debbie could hear about events as they developed. She also could hardly see out of the vehicle from her position, which required her to rely on what she heard. The continuous communications informed them that a large British convoy was in route from Tirana. Thankfully, the Pierces were picked up from Rinas, the airport, where they had mistakenly been left. They were able to join the convoy there.

Praise the Lord for radio communication. Otherwise, no one would have known about the Pierces, Roger, Nicki and baby James, being stranded at a closed airport. Dave Fyock, at the AEP in Tirana, and the Millners, John and Joanna, on the mountain in Kruja, worked tirelessly all day relaying messages. They also extended the range of our line-of-sight VHF radios. The Lord provided! It was really with His help that we had made it this far in to the day. Now, around one hundred fifty expatriates, comprised of missionaries from numerous countries, had been brought through seemingly random routes to this place.

REFUGE

There was also a group of Albanians standing near Debbie's window. They hoped to be able to tag along when we were taken out. None of us were feeling too cozy with the Albanians at the moment, so we seized the opportunity to tell one of them, with a cigarette, to move away from the vehicle. The smoke was going straight in to Debbie. We knew all this trouble wasn't these particular Albanians fault, but we our feelings weren't particularly ministerial at that moment.

I understood the group's anxiety, but I didn't like just dropping Debbie off and running to secure the vehicles. Duty bound, I took the driver's seat, and Jorge jumped in the passenger's side. We drove outside to the street, picked up the Zimmerly's Mitsubishi and delivered the vehicles to our friends in town. No one else was interested in going with us, and Glenn Zimmerly was satisfied to remain in the relative stability of the dock. Alone, we headed out.

There were five vehicles that needed refuge. We made arrangements for two. Paul gave his car to an Albanian believer who promised to care for it until he returned, whenever that might be. The fourth vehicle belonged to Bethany Christian Services. Their van joined our convoy earlier in the day when we were downtown trying to buy tickets for the ferry. The fifth car, an Albanian couple with a ten-month old baby recently born in America, was following the Bethany van. Needless to say, they were excited to leave the country.

Jorge and I drove away with our two vehicles, while Paul talked to the man about his car. The other vehicles were exposed to the forces that be. Left on the dock, vehicles would go home with a new owner, which is what happened to the Bethany vehicle. The fifth car disappeared and I never knew if it was taken or if the couple took it somewhere safer.

We felt duty-bound to protect mission property if we could. Obviously, people are more important, but we didn't want to just disregard the sacrifice of the believers that donated money to provide us with such a tool. The British convoy was left to the scavengers, but they were government vehicles and of no further use once they got their folks to the rescue point.

By this time, it was about 4:30 p.m. Following the most recent pattern around the country, when the shooting began, the police became invisible. All of their normal posts became empty. That made it possible for us to drive north inside the port and cross out into the city about a kilometer from our destination.

There were few people out on the streets without weapons. Fortunately, we drove straight to our goal without any difficulties. We grabbed a few things out of the vehicles and darted the six flights of stairs to alert our friends of our arrival. The husband was home by now, so he and his wife came down with us where we gave them the keys and documents. They solicited help, from some of their neighbors who happened to be coming by at that moment, carrying our luggage. There were two guitars, school files, luggage, boots and other miscellaneous items in the cars that needed to go up to their apartment.

We trusted them without reservation, because we knew the mother and daughter very well. If we are unable to return to Albania, then we were happy for this Christian family to have these possessions. It was useless to us at this point. Anarchic bandits were hardly worthy to enjoy these worldly possessions, as far as we were concerned, and we felt fortunate not to have to leave these things for the vultures. We hugged their necks and headed back toward the dock on foot. Even though we felt reasonably sure the gunfire nearby wasn't directed at us, we walked quickly. Half bent over and acutely tuned to all the possible indicators that might signal that we were mistaken.

It was a long several hundred meters across the vacant lot and down the railroad tracks. We briefly relaxed, upon entering the port area through a breech in the wall; only to see groups of people leaving the scene with their bounty. They had windshields carefully steadied on shopping buggies heading in one direction and two guys carrying a refrigerator in another. Momentarily, I wondered where the shopping buggy came from.

Finally, we made it back. We breathed a sigh of relief to be at the port with the group. We did everything we could do, and that was all we could do. Now, it was to move on to the next phase, whatever that was. I went straight to where Debbie was to let her know I was back. Patti Kadel was right there helping Debbie. She was a real God-send.

I stood outside Debbie's window, as close as the crowd next

to the car would let me. The fact that they were in my way was annoying. I didn't care whether they went with us. I didn't feel like coping with their cigarette smoke, and I didn't want to listen to them pleading their case as to why they should go. It was nearly dark on a long, stressful day, and with the looming prospect of a prolonged, stressful night, I couldn't help but transfer my frustration to these Albanians standing nearby.

*Zoti do të ruajë daljet
dhe hyrjet e tua, tani dhe përjetë.
Psalmet 121:8 ALB*

*The LORD will watch over your coming
and going both now and forevermore.
Psalm 121:8*

VIII. Listening to the Spirit

At our return to the group, I went to Debbie and Jorge went looking for Mel and Venisius. Jorge's wife Hermelinda was very relieved to see Jorge return. Even though she was not at the van when Debbie got hurt, she was terrified about the possibility of it happening to their baby whom she held in her arms. Jorge sat down beside her to give her some comfort.

Only minutes before Jorge returned, Erin, our fourteen-year-old daughter went over to sit with Mel. She was sitting and crying on the ground as she leaned against the wall with her baby in her lap. There was space to sit on either side of Mel, but as Erin approached, she felt a strong impression to sit on Mel's right leaving room for Jorge to sit on the left. She made a mental note regarding that distinct feeling and sat down on a piece of cardboard on Mel's right.

Erin sat and tried to console Mel until Jorge came back to where they were. Having an open spot on Mel's left, Jorge sat down. They began to emote in Portuguese, and catch each other up with what was happening respectively. Jorge quickly focused on consoling Hermelinda. She was very frightened, emotional, but controlled. Debbie's wound had put her on edge about her safety and the baby's.

After a few minutes, Erin felt like she needed to get up and go join the Mennonite YES Team who had started singing some praise songs. She arose and walked away just before another bullet hit the ground right where she was sitting right beside Mel. Jorge reached over and picked up the slug from under the cardboard.

Hermelinda burst into inconsolable tears, and Jorge asked if she and the Venisius could sit in the car with Debbie. Debbie, although in discomfort, knew it was safer for Mel and the baby to be in the car with her. Venisius did well, and all three endured the waiting confined within the car.

When news of what happened went through the crowd, it scared everyone and the group moved closer to the two parked cars. Erin and the YES Team continued singing all kinds of hymns, some in English and some in Shqip. Kristen and Erin sang a duet for the song "We want to see Jesus Lifted High" in Albanian, which added a serendipitous moment.

The singing relieved some of the tension and drew a crowd. A few Albanian believers came up to meet us, and they told us that they knew Genta, one of our church members from Lezha. Another one of the Albanians told of how he went to the Youth With A Mission's Discipleship Training School (DTS) with Fatjoni, one of the young leaders and interpreters in our church. This positive interaction began to rejuvenate an element of calm to an otherwise waning day.

Por, kur të vijë ai, Fryma e së vërtetës,
ai do t'ju prijë në çdo të vërtetë,
sepse ai nuk do të flasë nga vetja,
por do të thotë gjitha ato gjëra që ka dëgjuar
dhe do t'ju kumtojë gjërat që do vijnë.
Gjoni 16:13 ALB

But when he, the Spirit of truth, comes,
he will guide you into all truth.
He will not speak on his own;
he will speak only what he hears,
and he will tell you what is yet to come.
John 16:13

IX. You're on your own

Brian Smith was a helicopter pilot. We stood outside the car and spoke about his earlier discussions with an Italian diplomat, who was there on the dock, and a British Representative about an evacuation plan. We saw several helicopters across the bay, south of Durrës. Brian pointed out they were definitely American helicopters and called them by name. We thought maybe they were coming to get us, but their route was strange if they were bound for us. But, who knows what the military tact might be?

They never came for us, but went on into Tirana. We knew several countries had military vessels off the coast of Albania. We'd all been following the BBC reports on the HF radio for weeks. The circle of communication continued for hours between the Italian diplomat, a British representative, Rome, Brussels, the ships' captains, and the embassies. At one point, we were expecting helicopters to evacuate us. At another, it was landing craft. We weren't picky, just ready for someone to show up.

The American Embassy had an organized way to track where the Americans were in the country. A volunteer in an area was designated the warden. Their responsibility was to inventory and notify the embassy of all the Americans living in that area. If any information needed to flow from the embassy, then it could go through the warden. I was the warden for Lezha.

Dave Fyock was in contact with the various embassies throughout the day. He tried to relay adequate information to them about their nationals on the dock and to encourage their involvement in a rescue. With so many nationalities involved, we thought that was in our favor to spur someone to help. We operated under the assumption that our embassy would find value in sixty-eight of its citizens stranded on the dock.

Around 5:00 pm, Dave got final word from the American Embassy, the call on the radio to give us a surprising update. He said, "They are formulating a plan, but you can't count on them doing anything today. Maybe tomorrow. You're on your own."

"You're on your own?" coarsely muffled the group.

Dave paused, and the emotion was palpable. We were all listening to the radio and could not believe our ears. All during the excitement and trauma of the day, I always felt confident that help was on the horizon. I had that sense of urgency to get ready. Having reached a seeming dead end, and needing to leave himself, David had prayer over the radio and signed off.

Open mouthed, no one said anything after David said, "Over and clear." The sixty-eight Americans, fifty-two Brits, forty plus Italians, and sixty to seventy others were stunned. Silently, all of us Americans felt betrayed by our own country, but we also felt totally secure in the arms of our Lord, Jesus the Christ. This situation forced our hand as believers. We only had faith to turn to since only God was dependable, but the rejection of the Embassy still lingered through the night.

The Italian and British diplomats who were with us continued to communicate with their contacts by cell phone. We were reassured to think there may be other options, primarily the Italian navy. This offered some tangible hope. The British Navy was in the Adriatic Sea as well, but would defer to the Italians. The countries with larger embassies were conducting aerial and amphibian rescues. All of the British nationals were on the dock, so I thought the British Navy would be a natural choice. But, since we were next door to Italy and the Italian diplomat at the dock with us was taking the lead, the Italians got the nod.

The waiting game continued.

Nuk do t'ju lë bonjakë, do të kthehem te ju.
Gjoni 14:18 ALB

I will not leave you as orphans; I will come to you.
John 14:18

X. God provided

While waiting, stunned from being abandoned by our own country, I stood pondering all that had happened. June Kropf came up and said, "You know that guy that helped show you the hospital?"

"Sure." I said unknowing of what she might be about to say.

"When Paul and he came back to the port, Paul called out the window to Jorge to take your passports back to the hospital. He then turned back to thank the man for helping…and he was gone."

"Gone?" I shuttered.

"Yes, disappeared! There wasn't any place to hide out in that large driveway. He was just gone!" June exclaimed.

As I tried to take that in to process, June said, "It's really impacted Paul."

"I guess so!" was all I could say. I quickly ran that whole memory through my mind.

"It had to be an angel! God is taking care of us." She finished in almost hushed tones, with an attitude of confidence. There was no surprise that God was in charge. We hugged as we praised God for his provision.

Several of us had commented on the fact that we felt God's hand over us, and we felt that strange inner peace. He was definitely taking care of us. Wow! An angel!

Word spread and someone commented to Katie that they would like to be able to see all the angels that were there protecting us. Katie said smiling, "Yeah, but it would probably scare us to death!"

Dhe unë po ju them: Kushdo që do të rrëfeje për mua përpara njerëzve, edhe Biri i njeriut do ta rrëfejë përpara engjëjve të Perëndisë.
Luka 12:8 ALB

I tell you, whoever acknowledges me before men, the Son of Man will also acknowledge him before the angels of God.
Luke 12:8

XI. Yesterday

Many Albanians had come to the port looking for a way out of the country. They were very scared and began to befriend the foreigners. One woman in particular stood by Debbie's window the whole day and evening. Several times she tried to engage Debbie by making mention of being alone and scared and that said she'd come from Shkodra just to get on the ferry and leave.

As the daylight was fading and darkness approached, I was hopeful that the Albanians would go home. They continued to stay and accumulate. I knew that this was to their advantage. Who would be able to differentiate nationalities during a rescue in the dark? Plus, considering all the vehicles being hot-wired and looted during the day, we wondered what the darkness held for us now that we were officially on our own.

Groups of Albanians began building fires and gathering around them for warmth. Inside the Land Rover, Debbie could see the glow of the fires and hear the sporadic gunfire. As she looked out the car window into the starlit sky, she studied the showers of tracer bullets streaking across the sky like fireworks. She thought of her conversation with some boys in the village yesterday. She asked them where all those bullets went when they were shot into the air.

"They just disappear." They confidently responded. They had observed that the tracers did go out in mid flight and assumed that was what bullets did as well. She knew that if they could see her wound, they would be relieved of their illusion. This memory leads Debbie to remember more of the events from yesterday. She spoke with her good friend Maria, a new believer, who came by as soon as she heard we were leaving. We delayed leaving so we could meet our congregation to encourage them, and it was almost time to go meet our church. Maria, previously named Faria, changed her name to be a Christian name when she became a Christian. She came from a nominally Muslim background, in the sense that, though considered Muslim, neither she nor her husband and family were practicing Muslims. In fact, they knew nothing whatsoever about Islam. Their family was identified with the Muslims during the communist years. Religion was illegal in Albania, but families with Muslim names were made to choose Muslim names for their children and the same for families with Christian names. Consequently, every family had a particular religious identity without any way to practice or to even learn about their assigned faith.

As Debbie and Maria stood there talking, we began to hear gunfire from across the mountain. Maria said excitedly, "That's the depot at Manatij. They've taken it". This was very close to Lezha and the closest we'd been to the anarchy to date. The ladies hugged and cried knowing our town was next. We told her we were almost ready to go to church, so she ran home to freshen up and tell the kids to stay in the house.

The air was tense as we left for town around 3:45 p.m. on Wednesday. At 4:00, we began our prayer meeting with a small group of believers gathered together at Kisha Baptiste Laimi i Mirë, The Good News Baptist Church. We circled to pray and talk about the situation. Jorge, Debbie and I reassured them of our love and continued commitment to them. It was a perfect time of prayer and the Holy Spirit provided sweet comfort in the midst of the enveloping unknown.

Near finishing with prayer, the gunfire began. Immediately, the Spirit quenched and our attention was returned to the moment. Several of the women had small children at home or playing outside, so we immediately disbanded. We shared longer and tighter than usual hugs sprinkled with tears. Not that we ever know what tomorrow holds, but when things are chaotic, tomorrow seems too far away.

As we were pulling away from church, Shaun's former soccer coach stopped us and said, "There's trouble in the road to the south. Go this way quickly," pointing to the north. Weapons were rapidly distributed to the villages and people scurried in to cover and on switched survival mode. Trucks were filled with sacks of flour and grain. Women and children raced indoors.

Our back door neighbors were in shock. They were our dear friends, Lule, Llesh, Pjetër, Marintje, Ledi, and Jeni. All were there, except Pjetër, with hugs and tears and blessings being given unsure of when we would meet again. Marintje's husband, Pjetër, was working with the tractor in another village, and naturally she became quite worried about his safe return home. As gunshots rang over our heads with people trying out their new weapons, Llesh, the patriarch of the family directed, "You must go in now. Hurry!"

Our landlords, Tonini and Rake, and their son, Aldi, came by to check on us and to make plans to secure the house. They were going to move back in temporarily until we returned. We watched some news and had a cup of coffee, while they put some essentials in the refrigerator and a loaf of bread in the oven. We secured plans to get the animals fed, especially Debbie's rabbits, New Zealand Whites. These rabbits were a good food source, and we were expecting two litters around Easter. Our cat, Rachel, whom we've had for more than three years, was also close to birthing her kittens. We were disturbed leaving so much incomplete.

While Tonini and Rake were there, a military officer came by to see if we wanted an automatic weapon for protection. We declined the offer, as did our landlords. Shortly after the landlords left, Shaun came in the living room, with one of our teen-aged neighbors close behind him, carrying a Kalashnikov. We jumped up and quickly made sure he kept it pointing up. It was loaded with a full clip and just having it in the room caused quite a stir. Shaun wanted to help protect the village and we wanted to yell "NO WAY!" We restrained ourselves and conveyed appreciation of the spirit prompting his request. We assured him we knew the villagers would like his ten-year-old help, but we were leaving. He accepted that and gave the rifle back to our friend, Kastriot, who quickly left to go outside and shoot into the air.

We then made contact via radio with Paul and June to make our final plan for our rendezvous in the morning. We would meet them, with their group of twelve and two vehicles, and activate our plan to head north to Montenegro to catch a ferry in Bar for Italy.

Everything was set, and we finished up our last bit of packing. Katie brought her valuables to our house, and we closed up her house. Just two doors down from ours, her house was burgled

Tuesday night and the perpetrator stole some jewelry. Now, it felt safer to have her with us. We spent a fitful night with gunfire all around.

Debbie's thoughts evolved to how beautiful and sunny this morning had been, even though we awoke to sporadic gunfire and visions of a very different day. A sudden noise redirected her back to the reality of the dock and how uncomfortable she was.

Sepse, kudo që dy a tre janë bashkuar
në emrin tim,
unë jam në mes të tyre."
Mateu 18:20 ALB

For where two or three have gathered together in
My name,
I am there in their midst.
Matthew 18:20

XII. They're Coming...maybe

The square, hard seats of an old Land Rover were almost unbearable to Debbie. As the pain medication dwindled, she was feeling her head more and she couldn't move or reposition her legs. Her body was screaming out to lie down and rest. All day, no one had eaten anything beyond miscellaneous crackers brought by some individuals for snacks; no anticipated needing meals. We all wished some enterprising Albanian would come by selling byreks or bread or anything. We were sure they'd make quite a profit. Someone gave a piece of bread to Debbie, and she had a difficult time chewing it. She commented on what an amazing number of muscles we must use to chew. She sucked on it to dissolve it in her mouth.

Everybody was tired, hungry, sleepy and miserable. There was no place to get comfortable. Debbie jokingly said, "I'm thankful to be alive and now I'm miserable too!" It had been a terribly long day and the babies were extremely agitated. No one had any clues as to when this would end, or how.

The British embassy cars, those that joined us after the Customs compound was raided, were all lost. One by one, as we watched, the cars were eroded by the mob. They were relieved of windshields and various parts before being hot-wired and whisked away. Others were taken completely intact. Several of the "new owners" came over to our crowd looking for the owner of their new car. They required the keys and papers. We thought this was nervy, but under these circumstances, they got what they wanted. The only pleasure gotten by the British was watching the thieves work on the British Representative's car. It had a special safety feature that prevented it from being hot-wired, so a group of men and boys literally worked all night long trying to start it.

We discussed what possible outcomes the revolt would have

had if it had been raining during the last month or so. At this point, it eased our minds to talk about anything, and we quickly concluded that we were glad it wasn't raining. It was a beautiful cool evening in the forties, Fahrenheit, with a slight breeze. Actually, it was a little cooler than desirable since most of us were dressed for airline or ferry travel and not camping. When we gleaned and re-gleaned our things, heavy coats got culled.

The coming of dark brought a mix of emotions. We were grateful it wasn't any colder or even rainy. We feared what the darkness would hold for our safety and for an increased difficulty of a hopeful rescue, even if in the dark. There was an air of disappointment that the rescue was so long in coming, while hours earlier we had seen helicopters come and go several times to the south. We resorted to a strange enjoyment of the light show put on by the many tracers shot into the night sky accompanied by the rattle of automatic gunfire. Fatigue was an ingredient that marbled through our mix of emotions. The long day with no comfortable place to stretch out was taking its toll.

The six or eight bonfires the Albanians built around the dock area made it seem a little like a very large camp out. It was intimidating at first, but later we were very glad for the warmth.

As it got later in the evening, some of the Albanians got rowdy, which put us expats on edge. We weren't sure what direction this bored restlessness might take. Most of the crowd had been on the dock for ten or twelve hours waiting for something to happen. Several times when things got tense, a group of missionaries would start singing a praise song or a hymn. Praising the Lord always provided calm.

I stood out on the perimeter, mostly in front of the vehicle with Debbie. The men gravitated to the outside of the group, actively in a role as protectors. I liked to think that monitoring the entry points into our area provided a brand of security for our families and friends. The singing provided us security as it put us at ease, in whatever language, English, Shqip, Korean, or anything else.

Several times we got false alarms that the troops were on their way. It kept us on our toes. One time it was helicopters, and another time it was landing craft. Each time, we would scurry to find our families and the group would organize as we'd been instructed.

The British were in a group. The Italians were gathered close and the AEP group was together. The Albanian Encouragement Project provided ministry to the mission organizations. It was a hub for mostly all of the evangelical Christian organizations in Albania. The AEP group had everyone that wasn't either Italian or British. We called our group the American group, I suppose because it was easier to say. The Americans were the largest part of that group, but it included people from more than ten other countries.

We had a plan. We were told when the time came, get on the ground and lay low until the area was secured. As soon as the Italian Marines landed and secured an area, the Italians would line up to go first. The Italian diplomat was first in line, with my family, Katie and me following closely. The rest of the Italians would follow us, the Americans were next, and the British would close off our line.

If there was room, then Albanians with visas would be allowed to come. This sounded relatively simple in a day lit world with the rule of law. In the middle of the night, it seemed a stretch shrouded in the context of a dark and chaotic dock, covered with thousands of emotional people, some even armed, experiencing their world fall apart.

Each time a rumored rescue didn't occur, a tremor of disappointment rumbled through the expats. It reminded us that we couldn't give into our fatigue and hunger just yet. We men turned our focus as sentries back to a new scan of the mob looking to preserve a tentative balance we'd observed thus far.

Once that balance was achieved again, my mind wandered to the events of these last few days, especially today. My mind darted from one event to another, but each thought was laced with the abandonment by the American embassy. I couldn't shake that feeling of betrayal. As the night wore on, we all became edgier and edgier.

At one point a suspicious group, out in the crowd that we'd been keeping our eyes on, all of a sudden turned their attention toward us foreigners. Like someone flipped a switch, they looked at us and in seeming unison bellowed, "There are the foreigners." Their intentions could not have suddenly been to come for fellowship.

Just as quickly as their attention turned to us, it was distracted away. Their group had no more than taken a step in our direction when out from the side came a call from the crowd. "They're looting in Tirana!" That announcement exposed their intentions, and they turned to head off toward Tirana and join the fray.

That experience reminded me how God was protecting us, and we were sure to give Him Thanks and Glory. No one knew exactly how much cash was on the dock, but it certainly was significant. Many, if not most, of the expats withdrew money when we suspected a need to leave. This group could have significantly upset the delicate balance on the dock, setting off a feeding frenzy that would have added to the trauma of the day.

Close by, a group of missionaries began to sing softly in the night. This surrounded us with a cloak of peace, as people became stilled. The smell of smoke and the crackling of the bonfires provided an ambiance to the light show of tracers and opera of automatic weapons in the distance. As we sat in audience to this dramatic event, I pondered what a surreal finale this was to our nearly four years in Albania. It was a challenging, but very rich experience for our family. We had grown closer to each other and especially to the Lord. We knew it would be hard to tell all the stories of just our first term as career missionaries. June was to mark our fourth year.

Dhe, si shkoi pak përpara, ra me fytyrë për tokë dhe lutej duke thënë: "Ati im, në qoftë se është e mundur, largoje prej meje këtë kupë; megjithatë, jo si dua unë, por si do ti."
Mateu 26:39 ALB

And He went a little beyond them,
and fell on His face and prayed, saying,
"My Father, if it is possible, let this cup pass from Me;
yet not as I will, but as You will.
Matthew 26:39

XIII. At home in the States

Back in the States, most people didn't know where Albania was and fewer yet knew anything was going on in Albania. Short pieces on CNN and National Public Radio (NPR) were giving accurate, but small sound bites of the situation in Albania. The six-hour time difference kept the information slightly behind reality, but paralleled the same evolution of thought we went through. When trying to conceal bad news, that delay was a good thing. We wanted to tell them what happened ourselves.

Our family was concerned, and had been for weeks, but we had assured them by phone as recently as two days ago, on Tuesday, that we were alright and the outlook was good for us in the north. Kiffin, Heather and Blerim, Heather's husband, didn't have a television in their apartment so they got all their news listening to NPR. They were going to Santa Fe College in Gainesville, Florida, and at the time trying to focus on their schoolwork through the distraction of our plight. The NPR report on Tuesday morning was more of the same story. The trouble was in the south and spreading, and the rebels were demanding the resignation of the President.

Kiffin heard the evening report and began to understand better what was happening. The program All Things Considered had a new element in their latest update, northern cities. Kiffin, Heather and Blerim were savvy regarding Albania and Albanian culture. They all lived there, and Blerim was Albanian. They knew the implications of what they were hearing.

When the host, Deborah Amos, said on Tuesday evening, "The uprising in Albania took a new turn today. Most of the unrest is in the Southern part of the country. But there are reports that people in some Northern towns have taken up arms stolen from arsenals and barracks." This message signaled a potential change in how safe our situation really was, and they knew it didn't bode well for us.

Later in the same report, NPR reporter, Sylvia Poggioli, made the following comments.

Up to now, the anti-Berisha uprising has been concentrated in the South. But today, there were reports of several places in the North where townspeople looted arsenals and barracks and taken up arms. But the reports were confusing, some suggesting that local townspeople simply wanted to take weapons for self-protection – panicked by sensational reports of a thus-far non-existent Southern rebel army on the rampage northward."

Nevertheless, northeastern Albania is the birthplace of President Berisha, and said to be home to many of his loyalists. And the reports from the North created panic here in Tirana, where rumors began circulating that heavily-armed Berisha loyalists were moving toward the capital to defend their increasingly isolated president.

The deteriorating situation in Albania appeared worrisome enough to some Western embassies to advise their nationals to leave the country.

This news report on NPR confirmed their worst fears. The news leading up to this day fueled Kiffin and Heather's minds and paranoia. Doris and Irvin Griner, Debbie's parents, were obviously very concerned, but Kiffin and Heather had extensive first-hand experience with Albania and its people. They had a fond love of the Albanian people, but a fonder love of family. They had a frightened and transparent view of what was inevitable for the days to come. But, being right was the last thing they wanted this particular week.

Blerim's parents lived in Tirana and even though he was concerned, he knew his father kept a close eye on what happened at times like this. Tomor, Blerim's father, was an interpreter for the Hungarian embassy so he had access to inside information if there was any to be had. They took this news as more than a "heads up." It was ominous. They immediately intensified their prayers for Albania and for us.

Then the call came that Debbie had been shot in the arm or the leg. No one is sure how the news landed, but it hit hard and coursed through the family wherever they happened to be like an electric shock. Pacing. Antsy steps, snagging the tightly woven carpet while talking almost constantly on the phone, were part of every conversation that came across the line that particular day. There had been concern at home for weeks, but concern had quickly evolved into anxiety.

In Florida, Kiffin, Heather, Blerim and Debbie's parents waited for clear news of the evacuation. All that came to them was incomplete and pieced together, and not at all coherent. Kiffin pondered this news for a moment, and then spoke out of frustration. "Mom was shot in the arm or the leg? Well, which was it? Is it not obvious to tell the difference between the two?" Apparently, family and friends were not the only things having a difficult time escaping Albania. Truth and information were held up as well.

In Kentucky, my brother Bob, in spite of his focused effort to get answers, was having little success. Everyone in the family was doing all they could. They were calling anyone they thought might be able to help or at least pray. My father said at one point of frustration with the lack of dependable information, "Even if it doesn't help, it at least helps us feel like we are doing everything we can do to help." My dad, Boyd, and his wife, Gloria, moved to Louisville a few years before to be near Bob and Kathy with their family of five children. My mother, Ruth Johnson, was living in western North Carolina where much of our extended family on her side lived. They were going through the same drill, and calling everyone they even barely knew trying to get clear information, as were my other brother, Alan, and sister, Joy.

Bob contacted everyone he could think of including Nathan Deal, a United States Congressman from Georgia. We all went to church with the Deals at First Baptist Church of Gainesville, Georgia, so we knew they would do everything they could to help. Even though Nathan got the run-around by the State Department too, his interest as a congressman may well be what motivated them to look for us behind the scenes; while publicly claiming to have evacuated us.

Bob called Dr. John Lee Taylor, the pastor of First Baptist, to get him to spread the word in the prayer chain. He also asked him to reach into his network to get some attention on this situation, which he gladly did. John Lee was involved in our calling to Albania since my first trip in May 1992. He and his wife, Dolores, were great encouragers and advocates for our mission work. Dr. Taylor, in fact, had put me in touch with Cecil Sherman and the people at CBF to begin the conversation that would result in our commission to the Albanian people group as agriculture missionaries. The Taylors and many of our friends in Georgia were doing all they could.

Bob and Kathy did a short interview on a local Louisville television station between their times of hounding the State Department. The family in several states had a burning passion to pry open help and support from every source they could find. Through practicing their creative problem solving, there was comfort awarded in the effort.

Kiffin and Heather predicted Albania's demise, and within 24 hours it had fallen completely. The intensity and helplessness escalated. The family at home could literally do nothing and this fueled their desire to do even more, but with futility. Call after call was made and answered. All of the family stateside was in a holding pattern waiting for truth to be set free and permitted to grace them with its transcendence. Time was encapsulated in what felt like amber. Every phone call reinforced frustration as it was answered with anticipation and deflated with no answers.

Jon Harwell, the children's teacher for two years, was back in the States going to school and not even aware Albania was in such a state. He received a call from James and Mary Bergey, from Virginia, telling him Debbie had been shot in the head. The Bergeys traveled to Albania several times to join the Mennonite missionaries and became our dear friends. It is unsure if Jon's call to Florida was the first time more accurate news of Debbie's wound arrived, but almost simultaneously, the collective rhythm of the family's heart skipped a beat. Now, maybe more accurate information, but not what they wanted to hear.

The State Department rep out right lied to Bob, or had reasonably bad information. He conveyed that the Ayers family was all evacuated on helicopters from the embassy in Tirana and that our names were on the list of evacuees. At one point, he told Bob that they could charge $10,000 per person for transportation expenses in helicopters. Stunned and exasperated Bob said, "You mean, I give this government nearly 40% of every dollar I earn, and you want to charge us for taking care of American citizens in crisis? Why do you even exist, if you are not concerned about the very people you are paid to protect?" Bob continued. "This is absurd. I'm going to file a complaint. What is your name and position?" Bob was about as steamed as he has ever been. Completely gob-smacked, Bob saw this conversation with the government employee as going no further, so he hung up.

The Associated Press and CNN couldn't provide much more information either, but the family kept calling them in hopes of keeping the subject in the news. No one wanted something else to pop up and sweep it away. Everyone felt that the more they heard what people wanted to know, the more they would keep it on the front burner. We knew that our safety was front and center in the lives of our family and friends throughout the entire crisis. We had no way of knowing how much they knew, but we had no doubt we were precious to them.

Përgjigja e ëmbël e fashit zemërimin,
por fjala therëse e nxit zemërimin.
Fjalët e urta 15:1 ALB

A gentle answer turns away wrath,
but a harsh word stirs up anger.
Proverbs 15:1

XIV. Best laid plans...
They're Coming

Finally, about midnight we heard some engines inbound out of the black dark. We got word it was really happening this time. Debbie got out of the car when we heard our plan was underway, so everyone laid low for a few more minutes until it finally began to happen.

"Stay in your groups. The troops will identify you by who is on the ground" were the explicit instructions. We arranged into our groups: Italians, Americans, British and Albanians with visas. We were to be evacuated in that order. Since Debbie was wounded, she was to get at the front of the Italian group, behind the diplomat. Katie, the kids and I were to go as well so the family would not be separated.

The landing craft, a typical assault craft like in World War II (LCA), took a long time to position at the dock. The roar of the engines alerted the city that something was taking place. These assault landing craft were capable of quiet, but they chose loud. All night long, I expected to suddenly see soldiers stealthily appear on the scene. I wondered why the boats came in with diesel engines blaring. They obviously weren't trying to sneak in to rescue us.

By the time the craft docked, probably a thousand Albanians or more had joined the already tenuous scene on the dock. Some came out of curiosity, but most came out of a desire to flee. No one could confidently predict how bad conditions would ultimately get in the country. Everyone sought refuge in one form or another.

When the roughly thirty soldiers came ashore, they found a situation far beyond their preparation. They were in their battle dress and very much looked the part, with face paint and all. The squad had an interesting mix of personalization in their appearance, much like the movies portray.

The Albanians crowded around the area lit by the boat's spotlights. As some of the soldiers spread out along the waterfront and down the wall to our right, others wrapped around the crowd to the left. This created three sides of a perimeter around the entire crowd. The Albanians also encircled the expats on three sides so no exit avoided going through the throng. We waited for the signal, in order to move along with the Italian citizens. The diplomat took Debbie by the hand and said, "Okay, let's go." Kristen held on to Debbie. I held on to Kristen with one hand and Shaun with the other. Erin held Shaun and Katie's hands.

I thought as we started out that the troops were either not ready or they were set up wrong. I wasn't combat trained, but it was obvious that we were being led right through a big group of Albanians, not isolated from them. I knew at that point what would happen next. I'd seen it so many times over the last three and a half years. The Albanians would push in from the sides, and try to blend and force the crowd forward. Almost immediately, it began to happen that way. There was no consolation here in being right.

Because we couldn't see the ground, we were being led straight toward our target, through the coals of earlier fires and up and over some large concrete objects and piles of debris. Finally, the diplomat and Debbie burst forth through the edge of the crowd right next to the officer in charge. The rest of us, still holding hands, were immobilized by the compression of the crowd trying to push through. The forward surge of the mob was closing down the space on the end of the dock encumbering the soldiers' work. They stood the danger of being literally pushed off the dock either into the boat or the water. The soldiers kept telling people to move back, and they would do for a moment. But, only to surge forward again like a current in the sea.

Debbie did not have her passport and the officer in charge was calling for it before he'd let them pass. I was screaming, but to no avail. No more than four meters away, I was trapped out of reach and could barely talk loud enough to be heard. We seemed to be in a stalemate. I still kept yelling to them that I had the passports and telling the crowd that they are my family and we needed to stay together. We were too tightly packed to get through, and I was just out of reach. Even if the crowd cared about our plan, no one could move.

The diplomat did some fast-talking, and the officer let that group go. During one of the lulls between surges, I maneuvered Shaun forward enough to take hold of Kristen who still had hold of Debbie. I figured that if only a few could get out, I'd rather it be Debbie and the twins. It didn't occur to me that this would require Debbie to be responsible for two ten-year-olds and her gunshot wound, but the consumption of the mob motivated safety first. They rushed over and boarded the landing craft.

Kristen dropped her ladybug bag during one of the crowd surges. Erin and Katie retrieved it as they came by it in the shuffle. About this time, I thought something was going to have to happen if the rest of us were going to get on the boat. I was concerned; Erin and Katie were out of reach behind me and locked tight in the push. The crowd separated us. Then, after taking another big surge toward the water, they backed the marines closer to the end of the dock.

It was very dark except for the bonfires on one side and a couple of lights behind the soldiers. You could barely see anyone's facial features. The people who were further from dockside were frantically rushing toward the boat. Erin had her passport in her back pocket, the passport bag and her book bag. Katie had my backpack, her two bags, Kristen's ladybug bag and Kristen's troll-troll sticking out the top of her jacket. Troll-Troll was a troll doll that was Kristen's traveling companion and security.

Earlier, Erin gave Kristen her jacket since she was well layered. Neither Shaun nor Debbie had a bag, since we doubled up our packing. Each of the twins had about four of Katie's t-shirts layered up to stay warm and conserve space. We tried to stick together, but the turbulence of the crowd was too rough and tumultuous.

There was a middle-aged Albanian woman clinging to Katie and Erin while they were holding hands trying to edge forward. Another lady carrying a baby rushed in from the side, and she ran into the girls knocking the ladybug bag out of Katie's hand. She couldn't reach down to pick it up in the crush of the crowd, but when the pressure released slightly, she leaned over to pick up the ladybug bag. The lady with the baby was standing on it. They asked her in English and Albanian to get off, but with only a blank stare in response. They even tried pulling it out from underneath her feet, but she wouldn't budge. They finally resorted to grabbing the bag forcefully. The crowd surged again like a wave in the ocean, and we could hardly remain standing this time.

After multiple warnings from the lieutenant in command, he'd finally had enough. I don't remember hearing an order due to all the crowd noise, but I was looking straight at the commanding officer. He swung his weapon from his shoulder with one smooth motion and began firing into the air directly over the heads of the people in the front. Simultaneously, the entire group of soldiers along the waterfront and down both sides began firing their weapons into the air and moving with the crowd as it turned to flee. I instinctively ducked down, but found I was close enough to feel the shavings from their automatic weapons on my face. Several soldiers stopped firing long enough to introduce scatter bombs into the crowd. This may have added to the effectiveness of their tactic, but it also fueled the chaos.

One exploded one or two meters from me straight in front of where I was leaning. The bright red bursts threw a huge sound, and didn't kick up sand or send anything flying. This action was effective for a few moments, but then caused a stampede over the missionaries who were down on the ground following instructions, waiting for their turn. A line of soldiers, while firing into the air forcing the people to move back, moved in to our left. The combination of lights, smoke of different colors, an arsenal of automatic weapons going off, explosions and people screaming resembled an action scene of a movie.

The explosions redirected parts of the stampede. One of the blasts caused the whole crowd to shift across from our left, especially where Erin and Katie were, behind my position. They were extremely frightened by soldiers rushing around firing their weapons and the erratic thrashing of the mob. Erin numbed at the wonder of whether this was the end. She put her book bag over her head as a shield for her face and could feel people messing around in her back pockets where she had her passport. Erin slapped their hands determined to protect her passport. We'd preached to the kids about how valuable our passports were on the black market, plus she knew that was a necessary element of our exit. The intensity of stimuli caused Erin to burst into tears, an emotion being wrestled closer to its edges within us all.

The soldiers continued to fire and backed up quickly toward their line along the waterfront. In an unusual manner, a group of Albanians cheered. We all felt fearful at that point because we didn't know what that response foreboded. It was a motivational cheer like at a football game, not the typical adrenaline release in battle. It felt so out of the character for this moment that it frightened us.

The people surged back toward the retreating marines and the water, which brought more gunfire as the marines backed off the dock and disappeared into the landing craft. The crowd, seemingly undaunted, rushed toward the water. People followed the soldiers over the edge into the boat like a rush of water over a cliff.

The boat left with the Italian diplomat, Debbie, Shaun and Kristen, and miscellaneous others, and we were left on the port. Everyone was praying through the whole event, which was the only thing that could calm our spirits.

As the boats pushed off and retreated toward the mouth of the harbor in the black of night, I thought they would go get reinforcements and return. I was resolved at least that Debbie and the twins got out and assumed we would soon get our turn. The stampede relieved the pressure where we were standing. And, although chaos reigned, we were fine.

As I stood up from my ducking position to look for Erin and Katie, I saw they were hunched over already headed back toward where we began. There was still considerable commotion after the rousing exit of the military. In the middle of this gun battle, I found myself next to an elderly couple standing timidly in the middle of the chaos. The husband had some papers in his hand, and his wife stood close to him with her arm tucked in his. They appeared to be unconscious of the fray that surrounded them. They looked apprehensive, confused and very much out of character for where they were. In darkness, the couple was only discernable by an ethereal glow of the bonfires.

He spoke to me in Albanian, "We have our papers. Where do we go?" I felt sorry for them that they were confused, and that their legal exit would be delayed. But, at that moment, I was annoyed that they seemed totally oblivious to the war scene we'd just experienced that essentially blocked my exit. All of a sudden, the accumulation of my day exploded, "I DON'T KNOW! This is for us! It's not for you!"

The couple, in spite of my rudeness said, "Thank you." As I turned and left them standing there stunned, I recognized that I obviously was struggling. I thought I was handling the stress well, but I never responded to Albanians like this, especially kind elderly Albanians. It broke my heart to be so brash. It especially broke my heart that I was unable to go apologize. The couple vanished into the cold, loud, chaotic night.

I saw that Erin and Katie were back where we began. So, I walked back over to join them. Everyone was trying to recompose themselves when we got back to the cars. The Mennonite group and the CBF group took the brunt of the stampede. We didn't even know about that until we regrouped. Several bags and two laptops were stolen, glasses crushed and everyone's nerves lay in ruins. Parents shielded their children, making it impossible to know in the dark everything that was stolen as the stampede ravaged by grabbing and thrashing. Fortunately, we could account for each person.

By this time and far from view, the landing crafts were beyond the breakwater, but still remained slightly audible. Suddenly, from the dark on the other side of the dock, out came a sustained automatic gun burst in the direction of the boat that had Debbie, Shaun, Kristen and the others. There was a short reply from one of the Italian weapons. Then it became calm, with an eerie tone of tension lingering in the frigid air.

*Ka shumë plane në zemrën e njeriut,
por vetëm plani i Zotit do të mbetet i pandryshuar.
Fjalët e urta 19:21 ALB*

*Many are the plans in a man's heart,
but it is the LORD's purpose that prevails.
Proverbs 19:21*

XV. Night apart on the ship

The group that made it out hurried down into the boat and was being told to stay down. It seemed to Debbie that a few more could have gotten onto the boat, but the soldiers began to rev the engines and pull away under a cacophony of gunfire. Kristen burst into tears and said, "What about my dad? My daddy! I don't want to leave him here and Erin and Katie."

They were concerned for all that were left. Then suddenly, they heard the crowd cheer followed by more gunfire. They began to pray harder than ever for the safety of the people in the port and for themselves. Debbie and the twins continued to receive gunfire, so the soldiers turned off all the lights on the boat and drove in a zigzag pattern. The soldiers continued to tell them to stay down!

Debbie said to the twins, "This all seems like a dream, doesn't it?"

"It seems like a nightmare to me!" Shaun retorted.

Debbie talked to them over the roar of the engines to reaffirm that God had protected us thus far, and we would have faith that He would continue to protect us. When they passed what seemed like the worst of it, the soldiers turned on the lights again. It was cold, but they finally felt safe.

The landing craft drove right up into the big ship like pulling a car into the garage. There was a doctor waiting to see Debbie. He took her to the infirmary, while someone else took the twins to wait in another area. The doctors unwrapped the bloody bandage on Debbie's head, cleaned around the wound and inspected the sutures. Then, they put on a new bandage. The medics proceeded to bag Debbie's whole head like a ham with a stretch net bag. Debbie thought to herself that this was the second "stunning" event in the last twelve hours. "Surely they won't leave me this way", she thought.

The Dr. proceeded to take a pair of scissors and instead of cutting eye and mouth holes, he cut a circle around Debbie's face. They gave her an antibiotic, and said that the way the Albanian doctor fixed it was a little strange, but it looked okay. One of the corpsmen escorted Debbie back to join the twins, and they went to the mess area for some hot chocolate and crackers. There, Debbie was able to mix up the antibiotic.

Debbie looked at the twins, who were staring back at her, and asked, "How does my head looked all bagged up?"

Simultaneously, they answered, "You don't want to know, Mom!"

Adequately forewarned, Debbie quickly found the scarf Patti gave her to wear and put it on to disguise the cured ham look. She didn't prefer the way she looked in a scarf, and had expressed previously that she did not make a good village girl. However, she did decide even the village-girl look was better than looking like a ham.

Some sailors took them to a dining area for women and children. It was more comfortable, and the children had some fruit cocktail and more crackers. Due to their hunger, everything tasted like the best food ever.

Finally, about 2:30 a.m., the women and children were taken down below decks to a bunk area. Just as Debbie got Shaun and Kristen situated and thought she could lie down, a man wanted her to help with his sick wife. Debbie couldn't communicate with him, because she didn't even recognize what language he was speaking. She felt bad that she couldn't explain she was just barely able to keep herself going. Debbie told him no and squeezed her head under the bunk. She restlessly tried to find a comfortable position. It felt good to lie down, even with continued disturbances of noise and soldiers coming around counting and checking for passports, which they didn't have.

Several British soldiers, looking for someone who spoke English, came down and talked with Debbie for a while about the situation at the port. They said the fog was too heavy to go back. Debbie was hopeful the rest of our crowd would have made it out, but it seemed doubtful until the fog cleared. Neither the Italians nor the

British, or anyone else for that matter, would make another attempt at the rescue until it cleared. The rescue mission was thwarted.

*Unë e kërkova Zotin, dhe ai m'u përgjigj
dhe më çliroi nga të gjitha tmerret e mia.
Psalmet 34:4 ALB*

*I sought the Lord, and He heard me,
and delivered me from all my fears.
Psalms 34:4*

XVI. Night apart on the dock

Some of the expats overheard some people talking about going and getting their guns and coming back, which alarmed us all. The situation at the dock had been more than the marines had anticipated, and it erupted into a riot that may have angered the locals enough to come take it out on us. Immediately, following the aborted evacuation attempt, the crowd on the dock significantly reduced to several hundred Albanian "onlookers". We intensified our already intense praying.

The armed throngs that could have appeared never appeared. Different groups of missionaries, from time to time, would sing quietly. Sometimes they would be in Korean, other times in English or Albanian. Each time, the tension of the situation would ease. The intimidating fires built earlier, provided respite as different ones of the missionary community became too chilled to stay put. They moved closer to the fires, hoping for hospitality and warmth.

The Albanians around the fires welcomed us in, and tension relaxed even more. It felt good to not feel aversion to the Albanians and to relax for a few minutes. We remained alert by the notion that reinforcements would return at any minute to resume the evacuation.

We stayed outside all night on what was a beautiful, but cold, March night. Occasional warnings to stay low because of a possible evacuation proved to be false alarms, but it kept us ready and awake. The Italian communiqué was gone, and luckily the British Representative had a phone. This was our only contact with the outside world. About three o'clock, the word came that fog was delaying the resumption of the rescue, and it most likely wouldn't happen until morning.

During the moments of our waiting and in the midst of our mental fatigue, we could only be introspective about our time in

Albania. We pondered our work and the direction of the country. I recalled my first visit to the country in 1992, a short two months after their first elected democratic president took office. I had conversation with a teacher named Teuta from the city of Laç. I had asked her how she liked their new democratic freedom. She said she didn't.

"Democracy caused my favorite place to flood," she said.

Looking puzzled and quite clueless, I asked, "to flood?"

"Yes," she said confidently, like she'd really thought it through. "The arrival of democracy caused our support systems to stop working. The pumping stations that kept our favorite beachside worker's camp dry stopped working, so our camp flooded."

I thought that tonight in the cold, this was a strange memory to flow through my mind. That particular experience was the first of many to come that defined the challenge facing Albania in their transition. This anarchic response to failed pyramid schemes prompting our flight, certainly wouldn't help.

Remembering Teuta's beach issue linked my thoughts to the beach in Shengjin. That was the beach nearest where we lived and the place our church performed baptisms. Baptisms were always a festive time. We had a time of testimony before the baptism in the Adriatic Sea. Afterwards, we had a picnic lunch and played on the beach through the afternoon.

Thinking about baptism quickly took my mind to the last time we'd had one. I was taught a lesson that was still very poignant in my memory. We woke the morning of the baptism to crashing thunder and pouring rain. I thought, "What a shame for it to be raining today. I guess we'll have to reschedule the baptism. We can't go to the beach in a thunderstorm."

We couldn't call on the phone so I had to dress and go to town to coordinate with our pastor. He said, "Let's ask the ladies that are being baptized if they want to postpone it."

We walked in the still-pouring rain over to the building where four of the five candidates were waiting. "Of course we want to be baptized today!" was their excited answer. We both smiled and agreed. I'm not sure about Jorge, but I was confident this was a bad idea. I didn't like the idea that we were just delaying the ladies' disappointment. It took two vanloads two trips each to get everyone out to the beach. The thunder and lightning and pouring rain continued throughout the whole process.

On the first load, the ladies rode with us in our van and they were exuberantly singing praise songs and praising God the whole five miles out to the coast. All the while, I was talking to God saying, "Lord, I know you are plenty capable of stopping the rain, but I feel presumptuous to ask for that just so MY schedule won't be disrupted. Making that request feels like we're testing you."

We dropped the first load in the rain. They all ran around looking for shelter to wait while we went for the second load. All the way back to town, I kept praying and apologizing for putting the Lord in an awkward position. We picked up the second load, and we headed back out to the beach. The closer we got, the more anxious I became. I knew in a few minutes we'd be in place to perform a baptism in the middle of a persistent and violent thunderstorm.

As I turned off the pavement onto the sandy access road to the beach, the rain began to let up and the sky lightened. It wasn't like the clouds completely parted and the storm went away, but as we got out of the vans to join our group, the rain stopped and just overhead, the clouds parted enough for a little blue to peek through.

I felt convicted that I had doubted. I rationalized that I hadn't, but I did not think God would accommodate our plan. I was compelled to cry, but I expressed it as praise in my walk out to the shoreline as the ladies began their testimonies. We went into the water and baptized the five ladies. Then we had a time of celebration and lunch, without the rain. As we loaded the last group to go home, there was a roll of thunder and before we got home, it was raining again.

I smiled to myself on the dock as these thoughts rushed through my mind. Why was I surprised? God came through so many times in my life, not just during these years in Albania. I fervently thanked Him for protecting us especially these last few days.

Erin was crouched over, without a jacket and freezing, waiting desperately for morning or rescue, whichever came first. The hooded sweatshirt and t-shirts were not enough for the temperature. She and Katie huddled together between the Land Rovers for warmth. Any sleep was sporadic and restless due to all the gunfire. Periodically,

Erin would look up and watch the tracer bullets filling the night sky. She thought, "Those are all the bullets I can see, but I hear so many more. Where are the others landing?"

At one point, we were all startled when the crackling bonfires and the drone of distant gunfire was interrupted by a prolonged blast of automatic fire from the top of the water tank just outside the wall behind us. The shooter was directly over our heads shooting out into the distance. Fortunately, he soon stopped shooting and climbed down from the tank to find a better vantage point.

Even attempting to remain ready, I had finally gone as far as I could go. About four o'clock, I couldn't force my body to stand up any more. I didn't want to abandon my post on the perimeter, so I sat down right where I was standing; at the right front headlight of the Land Rover in which Debbie had been sitting. I pulled my knees up, leaned against the corner of the bumper, folded my arms and put my head down. My assumption was that if things got rowdy, I'd be in the way and the commotion would wake me up. I felt like I should go back and check on Erin and Katie, but I knew they were among friends. I was paralyzed by my fatigue.

Erin later recounted, "During the night an Albanian man had a seizure and was hemorrhaging." I must have been focused on a different drama at the time or it was during my short nap.

We basically spent a long, cold night in duress at Durrës. Not long before sunrise, a few of us began to try to shake off our sluggishness and become as alert as possible. We knew that something would soon begin to happen. It would either be a rescue or a replay of last night's mob scene with unforeseen direction. Only this time would be in the daylight. Anarchy and boredom are strange bedfellows. We strongly hoped the rescue would come before the city awoke and came back to the dock. No doubt, we all were praying hard for the rescue and we were confident that many others around the world were praying as well.

As the morning began to light up, we got our first view of the dock. We looked around at the trashed area covered with disserted grey humps of ash that were bonfires and other mounds still smoldering. During the wee hours of the morning, fuel for the fires had become scarce. The fire tenders began to scavenge for anything that might burn. They threw shoe parts from the shoe assembly facility along with any loose items they could find to throw into the waning flames. That momentarily rejuvenated the flames, but it left a lingering putrid smoke that smelled bad and burned our eyes.

As different groups began to arise, they walked around collecting their things and preparing for whatever could happen next; a few people found articles that were taken during the stampede. The Mennonite YES Team found a backpack and an overnight bag, but the computers were gone, casualties of the stampede. One of the members, Dwayne, noticed that the camera case he was carrying at his side, was hit by a bullet some time during the night, so close to hitting him. Everyone nearby praised the Lord for another example of His protection.

One of the Albanians standing nearby told us that earlier in the night, he had felt something tug on his sleeve and then land in his hand. He looked down and saw a hole in his sleeve and a bullet in his hand. I couldn't explain the physics of that experience, but at that point, I didn't doubt it. There were lots of amazing things that happened on the dock. Even Kristen, at one point, was pushed as she heard something whiz by. She turned to see who had pushed her and no one was there. While we waited, people began sharing their stories.

Dhe kështu Abrahami,
duke pritur me durim, fitoi premtimin.
Hebrenjve 6:15 ALB

And so after waiting patiently,
Abraham received what was promised.
Hebrews 6:15

XVII. Reunited

About 7:15 a.m., the Italian marines returned. This time, they arrived with over a hundred men. The boats came in steadily and quietly right up to the pier, much like I expected them to have done last night. We didn't even detect that they were coming until they were inside the harbor breakwater.

There was no stampede, and no one rushed. I think everyone was numb with fatigue, and we certainly didn't want to alert the town folk. Even the hundred or so Albanians that stood tending the fires all night, calmly waited for what would happen. The group that worked all night trying to start the British representative's car was still intent on their goal and seemed uninterested that the foreigners were leaving. In the end, their persistence paid off because the British representative finally relinquished the keys as we boarded the LCAs.

The soldiers moved onto the dock and took position by forming two lines facing away from each other. We were told to walk between the lines, which everyone did in an orderly manner. They learned that lesson from the botched evacuation last night.

Families with children were called to the front and we went into the boat. I joined Erin and Katie, and we proceeded to the end of the line. Erin remained frightened from last night, and, frankly, we were all still jumpy. To Erin, all the soldiers and weapons were intimidating, but close by my side, she was able to relax.

The Italian's plan this time was to take everyone, even Albanians. The sorting would come later on the ship instead of trying to check passports and visas on the dock. The soldiers were quiet and efficient, and everyone followed their directions without discussion.

Entering the landing craft was tricky in the daylight. I realized then how difficult it was for Debbie and those rescued in the dark to enter safely. I thought back about the soldiers and the people I saw go over the edge into the boats. It was a seven or eight foot drop to the ribbed, metal floor of the craft from the dock. It could have been a very painful fall.

Erin kept looking over her shoulder back toward the dock. She had developed a real friendship with the Mennonite YES Team and she was watching to make sure they got on one of the boats. When she saw them coming onboard she relaxed noticeably.

We were all "happy campers" aboard the craft. They weren't comfortable. They weren't warm. What they were was a sight for sore eyes. Every missionary there was rejoicing and praising God for getting us through one of the longest nights of our lives. As we eased away from the dock, going from the harbor into the bay, we could feel the cooler air out over the Adriatic Sea. The fresh air was a wonderful change from the smoky air on the dock. The bright sun peaking over the mountains enhanced our mood, as it was herald to a new, beautiful day.

On the ship, Debbie tried to tell the soldier at the door she wanted to look for her husband and the rest of her family, but to no avail. The language barrier blocked any productive conversation, but certainly the soldier was under orders to keep the civilians in their quarters until otherwise notified.

Shortly, Debbie remembered her medicine and she showed the bottle to the guard and he let her go, with Shaun and Kristen close behind. She found a water fountain to take her medicine, and the three of them wandered off to look for anyone they might recognize.

At about that same time, our craft pulled into the bay of the ship. This ship was a troop carrier. It had an entry ramp in the stern, similar to a garage, where the landing craft could enter and let down their front gate. This created a ramp for functional access in and out of the craft. We were immediately separated into two groups, women and children on one side and men on the other. They checked our passports, and then led us into the interior of the ship where they were serving hot chocolate, crackers and fruit cocktail.

We barely snacked the day and night before, and certainly had no opportunity for a proper meal.

Debbie and the twins were in the passageway where we were led to get our hot chocolate and snacks. They were delighted to begin seeing people that looked familiar. We didn't know for sure if we were even on the same ship as Debbie and the twins, but I was looking for them the moment I got on the boat. I was right up on Shaun and Kristen before I saw them. "Where's Mom?" I asked them as we happily embraced. "She's right there!" Pointing to a lady in a scarf that I had walked right by. The scarf obscured my seeing her and in the crowded narrow passageway of the ship, she'd missed me as well. Praise God! Everyone was tired, hungry and cold, but now we were safely reunited. We spent the next while sharing stories of the night before and enjoying our hot beverages and scrumptious treats.

Keith from the YES Team came and sat down by Erin at the table and they talked about the experience. Katie sat at the end of the table, laid her head down and tried to get a little rest. While we were sitting there, Dave and Sandy Allison came by with their family. They were missionaries with the Church of the Nazarene. I knew they were on the dock, but hadn't visited with them at all during the ordeal. We had been friends for several years, so needless to say, I was glad they were alright.

Chris, the Allison's oldest son, and Erin greeted each other, but before they could compare notes, they were interrupted by a guy sitting beside her. I didn't know him, but he asked Erin where she was when the shooting began. She told him the short version of her story, and he added that someone from the crowd had trampled on his youngest daughter's face during the stampede. She had a bruise on her cheek that marked the event, and apparently, her six older sisters were unscathed.

A crowd of people gathered around Debbie while she told the story about her wound. She told us of a point when Shaun, Kristen and herself got on the small boat, and it was receiving gunfire. This reiterated the trauma of the moment, and Kristen, knowing we were not on the boat, burst into tears. It was nice to be able to hug and console each other as we began enjoying a happy ending to our experience.

REFUGE

After about three hours on the ship, they announced that we would be switching ships. We were all curious why, but we were at their mercy.

Kur një numër i madh shqetësimesh më mbysnin,
përdëllimet e tua më jepnin zemër.
Psalmet 94:19 ALB

In the multitude of my anxieties within me,
your comforts delight my soul.
Psalms 94:19

XVIII. Processing, Waiting, Planning

We gathered up our stuff and queued up near the ramp where we entered. They loaded us on the landing craft to move us to another identical ship about a mile away. As we filed into the craft, we noticed the Albanians were separated and guarded. They sat in a bunch off to the side. We felt sorry for them, but there was nothing we could actively do. We were too tired to do anything but pray for them and their country.

At the other ship, our craft entered once, but it was told to exit again. After zigzagging around the stern of the boat for about fifteen minutes, we headed back toward the ship. We could see people walking around up on the helicopter deck of the ship and hoped they would let us get up there. As we entered, we noticed TV cameras and still cameras on the deck above our entry point chronicling our entry. I assumed we'd be on the Italian evening news that night. We figured the cameras weren't ready so we had to go out and come back. No worries, we were elated to be there.

By the time we arrived at the second ship, it was about 10:30 a.m. After again separating into a man group and a women and children group, the men went through a thorough full-body and bag search before being ushered to passport control. It was a slow process, but once through, we could go relax somewhere in the large internal bay of the ship to wait and wait and wait with the approximately six hundred other expats being held in that room.

The women and children sat and watched as we went through the searches and passport control. Much to their delight, they didn't have to go through such scrutiny. They did feel a bit like refugees being separated from their groups and families. That feeling was short-lived because the Italians took the women and children downstairs to get beds and a bathroom. Erin made note of their time in the rooms being from 1:40 p.m. until 8:00 p.m.

Debbie and some of the ladies washed their hair. Everyone got a chance to freshen up and wash their face and hands. In addition to a well-earned nap, they were awarded some focaccia bread and boxed water. The bread was so good Erin had a banquet with about five pieces.

Back on the inner deck where the men stayed, we laid and sat and leaned the best we could out in the middle of the hard steel deck. We spent the time taking short naps and planning for when we got off the ship. We knew at some point the Italians would turn us loose and we'd need a plan.

I didn't think anyone back home knew anything about Debbie's wound, and I assumed they would have been alerted by the massive evacuations carried out by multiple nations. The large number of people that made it to the ship surprised me. I wondered where they all came from. I made plans with some from our group to immediately find a phone, call home and give them an update.

The sailors had set up several stations where we could get a hot beverage and some crackers. That helped curb our hunger as we waited, and the Italians were wise to keep the portions relatively small. That way, it didn't fill us enough to start an exodus to the restroom. The ship wasn't designed for "tourists," and it would have been chaotic if six hundred people needed to access the facilities, especially since they were located on a different deck.

The ship was vibrating because the engines were running. The whole time we were waiting around, we pictured ourselves steaming along toward Italy. Late in the afternoon, a naval officer came through the crowd and announced we would soon be getting underway toward Brindisi. All this time, we were sitting still out in the Adriatic Sea. I was gob-smacked, as the British would say. It had been over thirty-seven hours since we left our home in Lezha Thursday morning. We were more than ready to be in forward motion.

As that officer was announcing our soon departure, another officer in a flight jumpsuit walked up and they greeted each other like friends. The second officer was the commander of the helicopter unit that had been evacuating people from the soccer field near the Italian embassy in Tirana. We overheard him say they had to suspend the rescue the night before partly because of the fog, but the helicopters also became targets of the incessant shooting. He was saved by his flak jacket when a round came through the side of the chopper and hit him in the side. He expressed that it became too dangerous to fly.

"Well, you think? …with thousands of weapons shooting in the air?" Humorously pierced my mind.

When the women and children were called back upstairs, they found us and sat down. They waited as we finalized our plans for calling home, eating and staying, respectively. The announcement finally came over the loudspeaker that everyone would exit in three separate groups: Italians first, Europeans second and anyone else third.

We qualified for the third group, so the crowd began to organize accordingly. The Brits, most of whom were our very good friends, got together to put on neckties and unfurled a large British flag. We Americans just had to smile and shake our heads. Who thought to pack a tie? While we scoffed a little at the pretentious Brits, we were impressed with their organization. Their government handled the evacuation by sending someone into the country to collect and escort their countrymen to safety, in whatever form that took. Still impressed, we thought the ties and the giant flag were a little over the top.

Along during the afternoon, the doctors on the ship wanted to see Debbie's head so we went up to the clinic for a while. She'd been seen on the other ship, but like a chain of custody, these doctors wanted to verify Debbie's condition. Everything looked good to them, but they wanted her to get an x-ray when we reached port in Brindisi to be sure. Soon, it was all arranged.

The plan to leave the ship changed to everyone exiting at one time. The media arrived outside the ship and wanted everyone to come out as a large mass. Just because of this, we ended up waiting an extra hour and a half inside the ship for them to get situated.

As we neared Brindisi, we confirmed our plans with friends from Switzerland that had connections with a nearby Christian retreat. Then, during our last hour or so on board, we double-checked our plans with the camp, because we heard a rumor that the Americans were being offered a special deal. I wondered how credible that rumor could be on what was essentially a refugee boat. They supposedly were offering a warm meal and a variation on the customs and immigration routine. There was also some mention about hotels that we didn't totally understand. Part of that plan meant we wouldn't have to process with the rest of the six hundred foreigners that had been rescued, which sounded nice. What we didn't want was for that plan to interfere with our other plans to stay nearby with our friends.

Më bëj të ec në rrugën e urdhërimeve të tua,
sepse në to gjej kënaqësinë time.
Psalmet 119:35 ALB

Direct me in the path of your commands,
for there I find delight.
Psalm 119:35

XIX. You want us to do what? No thanks.

At the time we landed, we thought no one knew our specific location or condition. Our first order of business upon being released in Italy was to personally call home. The family needed to hear our voices. Our thought was that if Debbie could tell them about her wound, the impact would be softer. "Shot in the head" sounds harsh no matter how you say it. This made Debbie the right spokesperson to tell them when we found a phone. We assumed we would be let loose when we arrived in Italy, and we would go call straight away.

The notion of anonymity was dashed when, in the midst of the hundreds of evacuees coming across the gangplank out of the ship's lower hold, a woman was calling out. "Ayers, Ayers, Is anyone named Ayers?" Even though she was slightly more than a silhouette in the glare of the spot lights along the naval docks, I could tell she was overdressed for the occasion. In a strange way, it was like someone you don't know meeting you at the airport. Her presence told us people knew more about Debbie than we thought, so much for no one knowing she was shot. Something was going on for anyone to specifically look for us.

We had to walk straight to her, silhouetted by all these bright lights from the cameras flashing in our eyes. The woman was from the U.S. Consulate in Rome, or maybe it was Naples. She was dispatched to Brindisi to offer the Americans passage to Rome and beyond. First, we were to be taken to the local airport to go through Customs and Immigration foregoing the mob scene at the naval docks and to eat a "hot" meal. Our entire CBF team and some other Americans followed her toward a military school bus that was waiting nearby.

We were hurried through the strange glare of lights toward the bus, when a journalist stopped me for an interview. Unsure of whom she represented, I still found her suddenly there in front of me with her cameraman in tow. Erin was standing right beside me while holding Katie's hand. She asked some typical question that I wanted to respond with "well, duh!" After she got a little sound bite from me, she started to let us pass, but turned toward Katie. Katie ignored her and brushed by.

In the daze of our fatigue from the last few days, we got on the military gray school bus thinking we were sorted out for some special privilege, shorter processing and a hot meal. Upon mounting the lighted bus, the driver, sitting sideways in his seat, pointed to a cardboard box on the first seat and said, "Grab you a meal on your way by."

The box was filled with a variety of military MREs, Meals Ready to Eat. The olive green-ish, brown-ish package was unmistakable. Was this a sign that our idea of a "hot" meal was an illusion? How'd we get that idea anyway? At that point, in a manner of speaking, the fog began to clear. We began looking at each other quizzically as if we were suddenly aware of some sinister plot.

"What's going on here?" was the look I gave to Rick Shaw. I was interpreting this same question on his tired face. We didn't trust the embassy folks at this point so, we started asking questions of the lady from Rome or Naples or wherever she was from. To be honest, we didn't care at that point.

She began to inform us of a grand plan to take us from the airport by bus to Rome where we'd stay in a very nice hotel. The next day, the Embassy would get us to the airport and make sure we were on a flight back to the United States.

We had all been "hanging out" for almost a day and a half, so the thought of sitting on a bus for another eight hours to Rome held no appeal. For Debbie, the thought was a nightmare. Besides, leaving Brindisi at eleven o'clock at night for an eight-hour drive didn't leave much time in a "very nice hotel" before going to the airport. All of this undoubtedly would be at our expense.

The entire CBF team got up, gathered our stuff and headed off the bus. Shuffling down the isle of the bus felt strange, since we were tired and had only been on the bus for less than five minutes. Our exodus was clearly viewed as confrontational. The embassy lady's program was falling apart before her saucer-wide eyes. She awkwardly maneuvered across the uneven ground in her high heels to keep all sixteen of us from getting away.

In the half-light of a distant spot light, we watched each other's breath as the CBF team expressed our desires and plans to the lady. Going to Rome was not an option from our position. It was non-negotiable. We had a perfect place to stay locally, and so far, she had not offered us anything more attractive. Going to the airport was acceptable, if we could clear customs, get something to eat and go our way. The hot meal idea was dead by this point, and we were confused where that rumor came from in the first place, but at this point it was all right. The MREs were much better than being hungry, and in the end, we both compromised. And thankfully, the camp bus driver graciously agreed to meet us at the airport.

The State Department lady, for whom I wish I had a name, acted quickly after that conversation. I suppose to keep us on the bus. She was visibly relieved when we turned our entourage around and shuffled back onto the bus. Very soon, we were bumping away from the Naval Base toward the airport.

Since the busses of Americans were under State Department care, we were allowed to leave the port area and go to the airport to be processed by Immigration and Customs. The full light of the airport was a much better setting for processing than in the cold and dim light of the naval base with the other six hundred evacuees. The Lord is always good.

Walking out of the airport and carrying our few bags toward the camp bus felt great, like we had finally been freed from captivity. The lady from the State Department was satisfied because we agreed to come to the airport for passport control. We were happy she upheld her end of the agreement. She managed to find several other Americans who we didn't know that agreed to accept her offer of a bus ride to Rome and a "nice hotel". The CBF team felt like in some small way we had prevailed. We finally loaded on the bus for the camp. Living with the Albanians had made us a little feistier and more independent than we already were when we came to their country.

We ate an eclectic mix of MREs at the airport. I remember thinking how good they tasted, but Erin felt sick from the omelet-in-a-bag version she'd consumed. We were out of the grasp of anyone making demands on us and that was a relief. Plus, we were staying close to Albania. The evacuation had us all in an unusual emotional state. We were glad to be away from the turmoil, but we all wanted to stay nearby. We were across the Adriatic Sea, but emotionally we were in Albania.

Nuk ka as dituri, as zgjuarësi
dhe as këshillë kundër Zotit.
Fjalët e urta 21:30 ALB

There is no wisdom, no insight,
no plan that can succeed against the LORD.
Proverbs 21:30 NIV

XX. Refuge

The lights of the southeastern seaport town of Brindisi flashed by the bus, becoming fewer and fewer as the bus made its way from the airport to the countryside where the facility La Buono Novella di Brindisi was located. La Buono Novella, the Good News, was also a publishing house that printed the Bible in different languages. This was the Brindisi location of the organization. Before long, we were pulling into a nice facility, well equipped for the group of thirty plus that sought refuge here. The Mennonite group with about fifteen, our group of sixteen and a few others that joined us felt blessed to be somewhere safe where we could stretch out.

To our delight, the sweet ladies of the Italian church that met in the camp buildings had supper waiting for us. Man, oh man, what a blessing it was to come into a place unexpectedly after midnight to find a truly hot meal waiting. Hot soup and fresh bread never tasted so good. The surprise and the pleasure of that meal made a wonderful statement about the sacrificial love of those Italian brothers and sisters in Christ and about the loving grace of our Lord. The comfort of the warm Holy Spirit in that place was as much a blessing as the warm bread and bowls of soup.

We were assigned rooms after that great midnight meal. Erin roomed with Ricki Buesing from our CBF team. They bunked with June, Kendra, Katie, Sonja, Ingrid, Regina, and Lisa from the Mennonite team. Erin recounted in her journal that she slept in her burgundy stretch pants, two shirts, and the only pair of socks she got out of Albania with; "blue, thin, and with a hole in the bottom." We were all in bunk beds with various quantities of covers cocooning ourselves with whatever we had, and we slept like babies. When we awoke Saturday morning, March 15, we were basically already dressed. We felt much better after a good rest, but there was still the feeling of being out of place. So far, it was like being forced to take a vacation and sleep in your clothes.

A worship service was planned that morning, but Debbie had a doctor's appointment at the US Air Force base. She was disappointed that she would miss the time of worship with everyone, but as she removed her bloody clothes to ready herself, it all came rushing back over her. She knew she needed the group at that moment. She wanted desperately to participate in the catharsis of worship, but she had to go. Kathy Smith loaned Debbie her jacket and they hugged and cried briefly as Debbie left for the base. It broke my heart that she had to miss this time of worship that marked the beginning of healing.

During the service, everyone let loose and praised God for being alive and extended prayers of protection for those that still remained in Albania. Everyone was singing and crying, and hugging each other. We listened to stories of the Albanian believers from our church and testified to our faith that they would take over the church and maintain it indigenously. God had worked a true miracle that was maturing and growing our faith. The praise and prayer time brought our emotions even closer to the surface, and it felt good to cry. After the service, we embraced and thanked God for His mighty power.

We called home the first chance we got. Debbie talked to her dad first, letting her parents know she was alright. Information was scarce and conflicting back at home. At first, they thought Debbie had been shot in the arm or the leg. The family assumed that in the worst case, Debbie would be able to carry on without a leg or arm. Later, the update included more accurate information about where she had been shot, but no details as to the seriousness. It's not hard to imagine what the family and friends thought when they heard she'd been shot in the head. It's very hard to soft-peddle that kind of information.

The information received by the family was against the backdrop of the month of news reports outlining the volatile situation in Albania. It didn't matter that all the trouble, until the last two days, was in the southern parts of the country. The northern part of the country where we lived was more calm than usual the whole time the south had been in anarchy. The family at home was obviously very concerned and it felt great to finally talk to them and put them at relative ease.

Don and Helen McNeely were dispatched by CBF to meet up with the team and facilitate our transitions. The State Department told them we had all been sent to Rome so they changed their flight from the Puglia area of Bari/Brindisi to Rome only to find out that we were not in Rome. Our first contact with them was when they found us by phone the next day. They were in Rome trying to find us. Once they located us, they made arrangements to fly to the Puglia Regional Airport closest to where we were. While we were at the airport to meet them, we rented cars so our team could get around.

It was nice having the McNeelys there with us. Don and Helen were seasoned missionaries that had themselves endured a number of trying experiences on the mission field. They had a wonderful way of making you feel cared for and loved. We didn't really know how wounded we were emotionally until we were able to process our experience and try to regain normalcy.

After a couple of days at the camp, the different groups went their separate ways. The Mennonites moved to another camp north of Bari while they sorted out their next steps. Their camp was fittingly named Il Refugio, the Refuge. Our CBF team left Sunday afternoon, March 16, to drive to Mottola about an hour and half away. We stayed in the largest Baptist church in Italy. It had plenty of space to house our team.

We hugged our close Mennonite, Swiss and Italian friends, had prayer and went our ways. It was a welcomed, but bitter sweet, next step in getting on with whatever was next in our missionary life. We drove away from our Albania home thinking we'd be gone two or three weeks. The experiences of the last several days had taken us into a time warp, which left us unable to anticipate when we'd go back, and in some ways, how to go forward. We knew life in Albania would be forever changed.

Don and Helen McNeeley stayed with us in Mottola. They helped provide communication home and linkage with the CBF office in Atlanta. It was such a relief to speak directly with our family back home. We had a soothing conversation with Dr. Keith Parks, the head of CBF missions. Dr. Parks was like our mission "daddy."

We left Mottola on Sunday morning, March 23. The families flew to Prague, Czech Republic by way of Rome and Frankfurt. The Buesings and Katie Dobbs had gone ahead of the rest of us on Thursday, March 20. Much of our time in Mottola was spent quietly, individually or in groups, talking or journaling.

That week was a great time of reflection and the wonderful members at the Baptist church were warm and amazing. They didn't have a pastor, but the church was fully functioning with lay leadership. They even had a mission church they were nurturing in another city. The people there provided a safe, loving environment for us to further heal. The church members gave us plenty of space to be introspective, while at the same time provided us with the doting attention for which Italian mothers are so well known.

Different church members would make food or invite us out. One day, we went down to the beach not far from Taranto. One church family had a beach house with an outdoor stone oven. We walked on the beach, though too cold to swim, and then enjoyed some focaccia bread baked in their oven. It was a wonderful diversion for all of us. Our emotions were still very close to the surface and if conversation worked its way around to Albania, we would get choked up and have to change the subject. It appeared that going back into Albania proper would not be advisable for a while.

Our organization wanted to bring the whole team together at the seminary in Prague, where we congregated for Europe-wide meetings. During that time, we would meet with a crisis counselor and discuss the next steps for the team. In Prague, Milton Womack was brought in from the States to be our counselor.

Milton did a great job with all of us, and the kids especially loved him. His specialty was post-traumatic counseling for children. Milton met with us individually, as couples, as families and spent plenty of time with the children. It was very helpful to have a knowledgeable third party to guide us through our healing process.

One of his counsel points was to not let our evacuation be "the" defining moment of our life. It absolutely was "a" defining moment, but not "the" defining moment. He had us talk about our experience and write it down. Milton also had us draw a time line of our individual life, putting points on the line noting significant milestones of our life. He instructed us to make a similar mark on the line that represented our traumatic exit from Albania. When we had finished, he had us ponder our timeline, making note that the "Albanian Evacuation" dot was one dot among many. I've applied that technique many times since then in an effort to weigh the impact of a situation, and to also be encouraged by its potential brevity.

Zoti është kështjella ime, fortesa ime dhe çliruesi im,
Perëndia im, shkëmbi im ku gjej strehë, mburoja ime, fuqia e
shpëtimit tim, streha ime e i lartë.
Psalmet 18:2 ALB

The LORD is my rock and my fortress and my deliverer,
My God, my rock, in whom I take refuge;
My shield and the horn of my salvation, my stronghold.
Psalms 18:2

After Words

It wasn't until I called home, finally getting through from the Christian facility, La Buono Novella, that our families had the true story of what happened. At first, Kiffin thought that I had called from the Navy vessel, but it was from the shore after we arrived in Brindisi, Italy. It was such a relief to Debbie and me to hear family voices and report in person. They expressed intense reassurance to hear our voices confirming a successful escape from Albania.

Reminiscent of his childhood when he wanted to track down and hurt the person that hit our dog in the street, Kiffin's first reaction to the news his mom was wounded was the desire to find the perpetrator of such violence to his mother. He quelled that emotion when I told him that all I could do when it happened was hold Debbie and pray we could get to the hospital in time to stop the bleeding. Kiffin had to check himself. He realized he needed to balance reality and hypotheticals to what really matters, and, for this tumultuous situation, that is moving forward towards healing physically and emotionally. No blame could be assigned, and holding on to a grudge toward the Albanians was not effective or beneficial. Debbie's healing and the safe return of the family was the remaining focus.

No doubt, all our extended family were relieved that we were on our way to a refuge that would provide an opportunity to mend before returning to the States. Even though we were unable to shield them from the initial shock of Debbie's injury, it felt great to be able to pass that milestone of communicating in person the truth and the good news. The good news spread quickly back in the States.

The British government arranged for a charter flight to meet their folks at the Brindisi airport and return them to the United

Kingdom.

The Mennonite YES Team went back home after several months at Il Refugio. Paul and June stayed on there during that time and worked with the ministries in southeastern Italy. When things settled somewhat in Albania, they went back to their church in Lezha. After some negotiations, they located their vehicle and essentially repurchased it from the person who was keeping it for them.

During the six weeks the CBF team was in Prague, the men of the team were sent out in pairs to survey the need to work with Albanians in the peripheral countries on the Balkan side and in Italy. Tony Buesing and I felt fortunate to be sent to the Italian side. Rick Shaw and Darrell Smith went to the Balkan side. Many Albanians had fled the country and our task was to see if our team could be of any help with those displaced peoples.

For three weeks, each pair traveled around researching the need for our help. We had the language and cultural experience and wanted to help. Darrell and Rick started looking in Skopje, Macedonia, where many ethnic Albanians already lived. They ventured into Kosova, Greece and Bulgaria and determined those countries were not being overwhelmed with displaced peoples.

Tony and I traveled all over Italy visiting temporary camps that had been set up by the Italian government. In every case, the Albanians were being cared for even though they had restricted movement. Naturally, since they were illegal aliens, they couldn't just wander around. There were a number of Christian NGOs, Catholic and Protestant, visiting the camps and providing the Italian authorities with some welcomed hands-on support. We found some of our friends from Lezha in one of the camps and they seemed very satisfied with the treatment they had received and the food. Their main complaint was boredom, but thankful that that was mitigated by the NGO volunteers that came around to visit.

We saw demonstrated time after time how resourceful the Albanians are. Whenever we rode a bus or a train or walked around, we would listen for the Albanian language. Several times, we heard it quietly spoken. I would say something to them in Albanian and they would immediately jump into Italian and say they didn't understand a thing we were saying. As for looks, the Albanians can blend with the Italians extremely well. We determined there was no pressing need for our team to get involved.

Our family was so close to going back to the States for Home Assignment that CBF told us to come on home. We got home to the States in the first part of May 1997. The rest of the team moved their base of operation from Albania to Macedonia.

In June, Darrell Smith and I met in Albania to collect and distribute our things and recover as much as we could from his house in Tirana and ours in Lezha. We had to arrange a military escort to go to our house since the country was still fairly unstable outside of the main cities. What I didn't give away there, I carried by plane to Bari, Italy and took to Il Refugio where the Mennonites were staying. One of the things I recovered was a guitar that belonged to one of the YES Team members, and I knew he'd love to get it back. I was also able to recover my guitar.

Even after two trips into the country to locate them, the two CBF vehicles were not recovered. Our VW van was seen several times. Some of our friends periodically contacted us, even while we were in Italy, to let us know they saw it. They would always ask if we wanted them to stop it, and take it back. We always declined their offer. We didn't want them to get hurt. Finally, after leaving for the second time, we heard that the man who kept it "safe" for us, and, who was mysteriously always out of the country when I was there to get the van, was found in a ditch shot multiple times. The van disappeared, and we stopped inquiring.

During our Home Assignment year, we were asked to take the directorship of a ministry in Homestead, Florida. We resisted because we felt our call to the Albanian people group. After some searching prayer, we felt as though the Lord was leading us to take on this new assignment.

On the move down to south Florida, in the dark moving truck on a long, lonely stretch of highway, I was still having a conversation with God about the decision to be reassigned away from the Albanians. In one of those moments when you know without a doubt that the Lord is speaking in spite of the silence, He simply said, "Just follow Me."

Kur një numër i madh shqetësimesh më mbysnin,
përdëllimet e tua më jepnin zemër.
Psalmet 94:19 ALB

When my anxious thoughts multiply within me, Your
consolations delight my soul.
Psalm 94:19

www.ingramcontent.com/pod-product-compliance
Lightning Source LLC
Chambersburg PA
CBHW051838040426
42447CB00006B/599